What others are saying about High Probability Sales Training:

"When I first walked into the High Probability Selling course I thought it was just another training. When I walked out I thought, 'Wow, that was really powerful. This is something I can apply to all aspects of my life, especially managing people.' I can honestly say that I've never been through a sales training program that had so much impact on me and the people that work for me. I knew right away that this was something really different and valuable. It gave people permission to be themselves...to be natural. My salespeople are more focused on what they're doing. They're more satisfied and more effective and they're not afraid to walk away. They enjoy their work more. The bottom line...they're more committed to themselves. They trust their instincts. During one recent three hour prospecting session, five of my salespeople set up thirty three appointments with high probability prospects. Those results speak for themselves." - **Lisa Gaeto, Sales Manager, Greater Atlantic Health Services**.

"There is no better way to prospect...An amazing difference before and after I took the workshops...Before High Probability Selling, I used to waste a tremendous amount of time meeting with and preparing proposals for prospects who never did business with me. After High Probability Selling, I spend most of my time working with prospects who become customers. I sold more long-term-care insurance than anyone else in my agency and I owe my present position to High Probability Selling." - **Steve Houser, CEO, Linsure, Inc.**

"High Prob has given me the strength to not buy any more sales books. High Prob gets to the marrow of what sales is really about. It took me off my knees. I got my self-respect back. I gave up my salesman's act and started dealing with people like a human being. I'm also now one of the top, long-term-care insurance producers in the country." - **Jerry Rubin, Independent Insurance Agent.**

"The High Probability Selling courses were extremely valuable and impacted not only the way I sell but the way I relate to people in other areas of my life as well. The first year after I took the courses I was the top producer in my company. This year I'm going to double last year's results. Without question those results are a function of being a high probability salesperson. I've learned how to effectively disqualify people, how to be direct and I don't waste time. High Probability Selling is one of the best experiences I've ever had both personally and professionally." - **Doris Theune, Vice-President, Meridian Asset Management.**

"High Probability Selling has a unique and really liberating perspective toward sales. Rather than the usual approach of trying to subtly pressure or manipulate the client into making a purchase, this new approach allows one the freedom to honestly assess the client's need for the product through a series of questions. Once this initial assessment phase is complete, the salesperson can arrive at a conclusion about whether or not to pursue the sales interaction further. There is an honesty and straightforwardness that aligns with my own inclination to be authentic and genuine. I feel that I establish a genuine relationship with the person I discuss my product with. I cannot recommend this program more highly." - **Ron Preston, Owner, Kudos Unlimited.**

"High Probability Selling is based on the same cornerstone as my company, Uncommon Courtesies... integrity, straightforwardness and respect for oneself and others. "Selling," as I understood it, ran counter to everything my company and I stand for. I couldn't tolerate the manufactured, convenient flattery. Having taken the High Probability courses, I see that this is not the way selling has to be. High Probability Selling has saved us untold energy and time, and renewed our enthusiasm. It is an integral part of the way we do business." -**Mary Mitchell, President, Uncommon Courtesies.**

"High Probability Selling made an incredible difference in the way I do business. I'm much more at ease calling prospects and meeting with them. For the first time in my life, I'm disqualifying people. I doubled my sales the first year after I took the High Probability Selling courses and I'm well on the way to doubling again this year. Learning High Probability Selling was like learning how to play tennis the right way after using my wrist for ten years." - **Jeff Delone, McAllister Financial Group.**

"I ask questions I never asked before and get the information I need - to know how to proceed. I'm able to discover exactly what it'll take to do business. I'm clearer about my market and what I have to offer. Prospecting is actually fun. I'm able to recognize High Probability Prospects and disqualify the rest. My sales went from $250,000 to $1,000,000 the year after I did the High Probability Selling courses. After my father took the course, our business really took off." - **Cliff Bassman, President, Promotions by Design.**

HIGH PROBABILITY® SELLING

Re-invents the Selling Process[SM]

JACQUES WERTH and
NICHOLAS E. RUBEN

ABBA PUBLISHING COMPANY
206 SOUTH CHANCELLOR STREET
NEWTOWN, PA 18940
800.394.7762
FAX 215.968.2983

Library of Congress Catalog Card Number: 91-77261
ISBN   0-9631550-3-2

Published by:

Abba Publishing Company
206 S. Chancellor Street
Newtown, PA 18940 USA

Revised Third Edition.

Cover Design - Anne Todd-Rink

This book is printed in the United States of America.

ISBN   0-9631550-3-2

Table of Contents

CHAPTER ONE   1
A New Paradigm

CHAPTER TWO   7
A New Beginning

CHAPTER THREE   21
High Probability Selling & Traditional Selling:
A Comparison

CHAPTER FOUR   34
High Probability Selling Applied:
Some New Concepts

CHAPTER FIVE   51
High Probability Prospecting

CHAPTER SIX   71
Target Marketing:
Identifying Niche Markets

CHAPTER SEVEN   83
Establishing a Relationship

CHAPTER EIGHT   99
Discovery/Dis-Qualification

CHAPTER NINE   113
High Probability Closing

CHAPTER TEN   125
Some Fine Points

CHAPTER ELEVEN   137
Conditions Of Satisfaction and Some Review

CHAPTER TWELVE   153
A Complete High Probability Sale

ACKNOWLEDGMENTS

Many people made valuable contributions to this book. First among them, in terms of overall impact, was our friend and business partner, Anthony Loscalzo. His early comments helped shape the structure of the book and his ongoing insightful contributions significantly strengthened the flow and content. For everything, Tony, thank you very much.

Gerald Kaplan, M.D., Esq., made major ongoing editorial contributions to the flow and content of this book. Gerry, thank you for the huge amount of time you spent assisting us.

Barton Pasternak's final editing significantly improved the quality of this book. Bart, thank you for your help.

We sincerely thank all the other fine people who made contributions to this book.

SPECIAL ACKNOWLEDGMENT

Without you, Jacques, this would never have
happened. Thank you.

Nick

AUTHORS' NOTE

The story of Salvatore Esman's on-the-job training in High Probability Selling is obviously fictitious. A conversational format was chosen as an entertaining way to introduce the reader to entirely new and perhaps even radical concepts, by contemporary standards, about selling. This book gives you a sense of how and why High Probability Selling works.

There was no particular reason for selecting the packaging industry as the setting for the story. It just turned out that way. High Probability Selling applies to virtually every product or service.

This is not intended to be a how-to book or an all inclusive text. It is not likely you will become proficient in High Probability Selling merely by reading about it. Learning High Probability Selling generally requires about thirty-six hours of rigorous interactive classroom time and a desire to be better than pretty good at what you do.

High Probability Selling is not just for people who sell. The principles apply to anyone whose job deals with a product or service - including lawyers, real estate agents, consultants and entrepreneurs.

Whenever possible, the word salesperson or salespeople is used instead of using a specific gender. Where that word seemed awkward, the male pronoun was used. In those situations, for economy purposes alone, the word "he" appears as a substitute for "he/she."

INTRODUCTION

Why doesn't sales training work?

Why is it that most people who attend sales training courses and seminars show very little sustained improvement? Why doesn't modern sales training consistently produce successful salespeople?

Why is it that most sales training courses and seminars contain large doses of motivational psychology? Why is it that the sales profession is the largest user of motivational training? Is it coincidental that the next largest user is the armed forces? What is it that the armed forces and salespeople have in common that requires them to be the largest users of motivational training? How many carpenters, mechanics, CPA's, claims adjusters or veterinarians need to attend motivational seminars in order to do their jobs?

How many professions come with a built-in, constant fear of rejection and a reluctance to do the job? Why do approximately eighty percent of the people who enter the selling profession leave within the first few years? Why do so many who remain feel trapped or burned out in their jobs?

Why do most people avoid salespeople?

Is this all endemic to selling or is there something fundamental about how we sell that causes these problems? Could it be that "Selling as the Art of

Persuasion" is a concept whose time has come and gone?

Could it be that it's no longer profitable to persuade and convince a large enough percentage of prospects to buy what they don't already want?

We maintain that it's not, and, even worse, that the attempt to do so is destructive to salespeople as human beings.

We've re-invented the selling process from top to bottom.

Everything's changed. All the rules are different. Fear of rejection is no longer an issue. Resistance disappears. Relationships of mutual trust and respect develop naturally.

Self-esteem comes with the new territory. Salespeople have standards. Who they are as people and who they are when they're selling no longer have to be different.

X High Probability Selling trains salespeople to discover whether there is a mutually acceptable basis for doing business without using manipulative techniques. High Probability Selling is not an improvement on or a variation of any sales technique you know. It's a new paradigm that allows salespeople to sell with integrity and achieve outstanding results.

High Probability Selling takes salespeople off their knees and puts them back on their feet, with dignity, where they belong.

CHAPTER ONE

A New Paradigm

On the first day of our High Probability Selling workshop we ask the participants some questions about selling. After a few minutes of reserved responses people begin to shout out how they really feel. The following is typical of what we hear.

1. **What is selling?**
    Initial responses are pretty much textbook:
    "The fulfilling of needs, providing a service, pointing out benefits, the art of persuasion."

2. **What is your objective when you sell?**
    "Getting the prospect to buy, making money, closing the sale." The consensus objective ends up being **getting the prospect to buy.**

3. **What do you do to get the prospect to buy?**
    This is when things start to get interesting. At first, people say things like: "Educate them, promise them good service, get to know them, point out the benefits of dealing with me or my company." Then it starts to get a little down and dirty: "Convince them, pressure them, put down the competition, act like I'm their friend."

4. **What will you do to get the prospect to buy?**
    This is where things really break loose. Someone invariably yells out "anything" or "whatever it takes," and then the dam opens: "Scare them, beg, manipulate, con, stretch the truth (eventually someone says lie), be

insincere and unauthentic (pretend you like them, that you're interested in them and compliment them whenever possible), grovel, kiss ass, promise to be available at any time, turn myself inside out, be whatever they want me to be."

5. **How do your prospects feel when they're being sold?**
By this point some basic truths about the selling process are starting to surface: "Resistant, suspicious, resentful, scared, confused, hostile, like their intelligence is being insulted, pressured, like a piece of meat, hunted, vulnerable, abused." Once in a while a participant says their prospects feel good during the selling process. Those participants usually receive questioning looks from the other participants.

6. **How do you feel when you're selling?**
"Scared, vulnerable, like the prospect's in charge, like a supplicant, not good, lacking in self-respect, like I'm struggling, abused, violated, desperate, anxious, angry, pissed off." A minority say they feel good when they're selling, but as the workshop unfolds, most of them retreat from that position.

7. **How do you feel when you don't make the sale?**
"Lousy, hurt, rejected, frustrated, resentful, like a failure, angry."

8. **How do you feel at the end of a selling day in which you've made no sales?**
"Like a failure, there has to a be a better way to make a living, less than..., vulnerable, stressed, beat-up, drained."

9. **In our society is there a sense of trust or distrust of salespeople?** (This is a "Who is buried in Grant's tomb?" question if there ever was one.) Participants

typically smile and reply, "Distrust, of course."

10. **What causes sales resistance?**
     Participants usually give a number of causes for sales
     resistance: "Pressure, past experience, insincerity,
     begging." Then eventually someone says, "Selling."
     It's called sales resistance because SELLING CAUSES
     RESISTANCE. And every attempt to mask the selling
     objective causes more resistance.

What becomes crystal clear is that selling is a painful and
difficult process for buyers and sellers. So why is it like this?
Why is this the way it is?

Because the objective of selling as it's currently defined (the
current selling paradigm), is **to get the prospect to buy**.
Selling, by definition, is getting somebody to do something,
usually something they might not otherwise do. It implies any
conduct that can produce a sale, including convincing,
persuading or pressuring someone to buy from you. We call
this approach the paradigm of **Traditional Selling.**

When you feel someone is trying to get you to do what they
want you to do, the relationship, by definition, becomes
adversarial and by reflex you try to protect yourself. That's
where resistance, suspicion and hostility come from.
Traditional Selling, regardless of how it's cloaked, is hunter
versus prey.

Fish exist in a paradigm called water. Fish aren't aware of the
water because the water is constant and always there. There's
never any "not water." The water, however, shapes their
universe; how they move, how they eat, how they breathe and
how they act. Traditional Selling is to salespeople what water
is to fish.

WHAT IS A PARADIGM?

We don't think about paradigms. They're just there. They shape what we think, what we do and even define what's possible. A paradigm is the filter or lens you receive information through, the window you look through, without knowing you're looking through anything. Here are examples of paradigm shifts.

FLAT WORLD/ROUND WORLD
At one time people lived in a paradigm called flat world. No one talked about it being flat. It just **was** flat. And the paradigm, flat world, shaped what people thought and did. That paradigm kept exploration of the world to a minimum. Flat world defined what was possible and how it could be done.

Then, at some point, it was demonstrated that the earth was round. All of a sudden the rules were different. You could sail west and wind up back where you started. Everything changed. Geographical concepts were turned inside out, and new questions arose. For example, if the earth is round, why don't people fall off?

HUMORS/GERMS
At one time, state of the art medicine held that disease was caused by evil humors (vapors) in the air. All medical thinking, including diagnosis and treatment, was based on this premise.

When it was later suggested that disease was caused by invisible microbes called germs, the medical establishment was resistant at best, and hostile at worst. When the germ theory of disease was finally proven, all of a sudden all the rules were different. The new paradigm turned every experienced physician into a beginner.

NEWTONIAN PHYSICS/RELATIVITY THEORY

For many years Newtonian physics shaped scientific thinking and inquiry. Einstein conceived the theory of relativity and the equation $E = MC^2$ which radically altered fundamental principles of viewing the universe. Time, it turned out, was relative and space curved.

SOME OBSERVATIONS

New paradigms are not logical extensions of existing paradigms. They represent leaps of intuition. Round world doesn't logically follow from flat world. Germs don't follow from humors. The theory of Relativity didn't follow from Newtonian principles.

Until now, the premise (paradigm) that the salesperson's objective is **to get the prospect to buy** has been largely unexamined. As a matter of fact, paradigms, being generally invisible, rarely get examined. But paradigms shape and limit activity. As a result, efforts to improve sales techniques have consisted of devising new and better ways **to get the prospect to buy** and overcoming all the objections which arise in an adversarial environment.

HIGH PROBABILITY SELLING

High Probability Selling is a new paradigm for selling.

In High Probability Selling the paradigm shifts from getting the prospect to buy to determining whether there is a mutually acceptable basis for doing business.

As described above, when a paradigm shifts, everything shifts along with it. When you replace an existing paradigm with a new one, everything has to be reexamined, from top to bottom. You literally destroy the entire previous basis and all of its ideas and conclusions. That's a very unsettling and disturbing process. People have no place to hold a new paradigm because it doesn't fit inside the old one, and, in many cases, it invalidates it. In the past this kind of problem was solved by burning the proponent of the new paradigm at the stake. Now we just give them a real hard time.

The best way to get value from this book is to put aside every belief you have about selling. Don't filter this information through what you already know (your beliefs). Set those beliefs aside, especially those you are sure of, as you read this book. Remember, what you know about selling may be true in the old selling paradigm, but all the rules are different in the new one.

What follows is a story about an intelligent, hard working, but frustrated salesperson who learns the basics of High Probability Selling.

CHAPTER TWO

A New Beginning

Salvatore Esman had been in sales for seven years. Prior to getting into sales, he had worked in the art and then the printing and finishing departments of a medium-sized custom packaging manufacturer. While he was still in production, the company's sales manager recognized Sal's ambition and his gift of gab, and he suggested that Sal try selling. Sal accepted the suggestion because he felt he wanted to make the kind of money sales could offer.

Sal was trained to sell by two hard-hitting, aggressive, old pros. First, they had him attend a two-week training course given by one of the world's largest sales training companies. Then he attended a couple of seminar programs on his own, and read a couple of how-to books on technique and psychology.

Sal felt he would enjoy sales because he was a "people person." Unfortunately, his results did not match his enthusiasm. Of the twelve people in his sales department, Sal's performance was never better than average, and soon he became dissatisfied. In the past, he had excelled at most everything he tried, but after a few years in sales he began to feel "burned out." Sal thought he felt that way because of the intense discomfort he experienced when he had to press prospects to close. The only time he didn't feel "burned out" was during the two or three day period following a motivational seminar. So he bought some motivational tapes and listened to them in his car. The tapes seemed to get him "up," but soon the novelty wore off and he was back in the same old rut.

Sal was a hard worker who took good care of his customers. The problem was he didn't have enough of them. Calling on new prospects was his toughest challenge, mostly because it wasn't very rewarding. His sales manager often told him that he had to act more enthusiastic with prospects, and that he should learn to be more aggressive. His general manager told him he was not a strong closer and just needed to work harder. The department sent him to another sales training program that was supposed to cure "call reluctance" and the "fear of rejection." But the pattern never seemed to change. For a week or two he felt energized, but after that it was back to square one. What seemed new at first was really just a rehash of the same old stuff.

Sal's sales manager then decided to send him on some sales calls with their top three salespeople. Sal sat quietly and listened closely, but as far as he could tell there was little difference between what they did and what he did. One did a sharp, eye-catching demonstration, using striking and colorful materials. The second had a great sense of humor and a gregarious personality which he used with style. The third was incredibly aggressive.

All three were very convincing when demonstrating the benefits of the company's packaging products and services. They usually managed to deliver their complete presentation with a minimum of interruptions or objections, (something Sal had rarely been able to accomplish). Mainly, they seemed stronger than he could ever be. But even these apparent stars said there were periods when they too found it difficult to remain enthusiastic, energetic and aggressive. They admitted that sometimes prospects got angry during their presentations, and some didn't respond at all.

In so many words each of them said, "Sales is a game of

numbers. If you just go out and make enough calls, do it to the best of your ability, day after day, you'll get your share. And, if you work on your style and learn to handle the most common objections, your closing rate will improve. Then if you learn five or six good, strong closing techniques and use them consistently, you'll close even more. Those are the real answers to selling!"

The trouble was, Sal already knew all that. He was beginning to fear that he just didn't have the talent to be top-notch in sales, so he began thinking about getting out of sales and going back into production. The problem was, production jobs didn't pay what he wanted to earn. Eventually Sal found himself talking to an employment counselor who specialized in placements in the packaging industry. She suggested that before he gave up on selling, he should apply for a sales job with one of her clients, Wraparound Packaging Company (WPC). Feeling he had nothing to lose, Sal asked her to set up an interview.

During the preliminary interview with WPC's Assistant Sales Manager, Sal was asked if he was willing to take some written tests to determine his "personality profile," and his aptitude for WPC's approach to sales. He agreed and took the tests that same day. A few days later, WPC's Assistant Sales Manager called him for an interview with the company's sales executives. She told Sal he had scored quite well and they considered him a trainable candidate.

At the preliminary interview the Assistant Sales Manager had stressed that, if hired, Sal would have to learn how to sell "their way." When Sal asked what "their way" was, the Assistant Sales Manager told him a little about what she called High Probability Selling. Overall, he would have to learn how to spend his resources **only** on customers who needed and wanted what WPC had to sell; that learning High Probability Selling would not be easy, and toughest of all would be giving up most of his old ideas about selling. She said however that the rewards, both financial and emotional, would be well worth his effort. In other words, this was an opportunity to earn good money in a career he would enjoy.

Sal was understandably skeptical about what sounded like pretty extravagant claims. But, even if she were exaggerating, he felt he could only benefit by learning something new about selling. He suspected from experience that "High Probability Selling" was another sophisticated rehash of traditional sales psychology. But he was intrigued when the Assistant Sales Manager told him that empathy and respect for other people were the most important criteria for learning High Probability Selling, and that he had displayed those traits in his testing. As far as giving up what he already knew about selling... well, so what, a few days ago he was ready to quit altogether.

Sal started at WPC two weeks later. After a two-day orientation, he met the Vice-President of Sales and Marketing, Victor Preston (VP), who was going to do most of his training. Sal was concerned because VP's relaxed style just didn't fit his picture of a top-notch salesman.

At their first meeting, Sal asked Victor to describe High Probability Selling, but Victor said it was too soon for descriptions since people tend to fit new information into preconceived ideas. "With an approach as gentle and different as High Probability Selling," he said, "it's better to see it in action first, and learn the how's and why's later."

A few days later, Sal and VP made their first call together, visiting a multi-billion dollar consumer products manufacturer. VP told Sal that WPC had received their first order from this customer less than a year ago. Since that time they had become WPC's fourth largest customer, even though WPC had only a small portion of their packaging business.

Right before the meeting, VP told Sal to just observe what was going on and say nothing, even if it seemed that VP might be in need of help. When they arrived, they were taken to the buyer's office. After the introductions were completed, here's what happened:

The Buyer, Ann Kaufman, seemed to be annoyed. She opened the conversation by curtly saying that she was very busy and asking why they had come.

VP: You seem upset.

Ann: It has nothing to do with you. I'm in a bind because another vendor's late with a critical delivery.

VP: Perhaps we should come back at another time.

Ann: No, it's all right. There's nothing I can do about it now.

VP: You still seem upset.

Ann: I'm okay. Don't worry, I won't take it out on you.

VP: When we first began to do business with your company, you told me that in order to gain "Favored-Vendor" status, we'd have to deliver top-quality goods and be on time. So I know how important reliability is to you.

Ann: Yes, we've become the most profitable company in our field by reducing costs through minimizing inventories and rejects. To do that we have to rely heavily on our vendors. When a vendor delivers late or ships poor quality goods, we suffer losses that go way beyond the cost of that shipment. And when that happens, I become the focus of a lot of negative attention.

VP: Last week I found out WPC made your Favored Vendors' list. We appreciate the recognition.

Ann: We've been very pleased with your quality and on-time deliveries, so far. But at the moment I don't have any open requirements for the line you've been servicing.

VP: Do you want our packaging for any of your other lines?

Ann: Interesting you should say that. I've been having some problems with the packaging-suppliers for two of our other brands.

VP: Which brands?

Ann: Sun and Moon.

VP: What kind of problems?

Ann: Well, the Sun supplier is having quality problems, and the supplier for Moon hasn't been able to handle the volume.

VP: How serious are the problems?

Ann: In Sun's case, the supplier's been told to redo the art work and improve the quality. Unfortunately, I think their quality problems extend into production, too, so I'm really concerned. If we decide to deal with a new vendor, they'd have to come up with new art work of high quality to get that business.

VP: How much time is available to produce the new art work?

Ann: Not much. First, I'd have to have a quote and then have our product manager approve it.

VP: Is that something you want us to do?

Ann: Yes, if you can. The material type and package sizes are about the same as the Star line. Only the print variations are substantially different.

VP: All right. But I'll need to review the art work with your product manager, so that I know exactly what's required for the quote.

Ann: I'd rather not do it that way. I'd like to see your quote before we get the product manager involved.

VP: That's not how I work. I'm not willing to quote it twice. After we get all of the necessary information I'll quote it. That's why we need to talk to the product manager first. Is that okay with you... or not?

Ann: What you're saying makes sense. I'll call him to see if he can join us now.

Five minutes later the product manager for the Sun line arrived carrying samples of the current art work and packaging. After outlining his requirements, the product manager (PM) asked, "How long will it take you to provide new art work for these seventeen packages?"

VP: In order to minimize overtime costs in our art department it would be best to schedule the work as needed. Does that work for you?

PM: Yes, it does.

VP: How many packages do you need right away?

PM: We need four of them delivered within 5 weeks.

VP: If we just work on four, we can have the art work completed in a week. We can deliver the packaging four weeks after you approve the art work. That meets the five week delivery schedule you need. Is that what you want us to do?

PM: We already have the four packages on order with our current vendor, but I wouldn't mind duplicating the order. That way I double my chances of having acceptable packaging on hand by the time production is completed. Of course, that'll reduce my line's profitability for the quarter and have the same effect on my performance bonus. But if you come through, I'll be much better off in the long run.

VP: What would it take for you to be confident that we'll meet your requirements?

PM: If you can send me daily progress reports and copies of the art work in progress, that will help. I can't cancel the order to our current supplier, but, if you keep your end of the bargain, I promise you at least half my packaging requirements, even if the other supplier comes through. They've already messed us up too many times, so I have to have someone else I can depend on.

VP: We'll fax "proofs" to you every morning, since most of the work on the first four packages will be done on overtime. Is that what you want?

PM: Yes. Definitely.

VP: How much time would we have to prepare the remaining thirteen packages?

PM: Between eight weeks and fifteen weeks. I'll get you a copy of the schedule.

VP: We won't have any problem with the eight and fifteen week deliveries. Are you ready to make some commitments?

PM: What do you mean?

VP: I'm ready to make some commitments if you are.

PM: I guess that depends on the price. Ms. Kaufman's department handles that end initially. But the purchase ultimately comes out of my budget, so it'll come back to me for approval.

VP: Ms. Kaufman's already familiar with our pricing. We've done all the art work and packaging for your Star line. With Sun, only the colors and layouts are different. The price will be about the same. Assuming we can get a quote to her tomorrow, and that the price is in line, how soon can you approve the quote so she can release the order?

Ann: Their prices for Star have been in line, maybe a little higher than average.

PM: Price isn't the most important thing. I must have top-quality goods, on-time deliveries, no shortages and no more than two percent overages. If we agree on the price, I'll approve it tomorrow. Just don't miss delivery dates.

VP: Your company gave us "Favored Vendor" status last week. We got that because our quality has been first-rate and our deliveries have consistently been on time.

PM: I'm glad to hear that. But sometimes performance slips when a vendor takes on a bigger load.

VP: Is that something you want to talk about now?

PM: No. Time will tell.

VP: (Reading from notes he took during the meeting) We've covered your requirements for new art work and overall timing. We've agreed on the way we'll handle the delivery schedule for the packaging. We've agreed that I'll have our written quote here tomorrow, and the price will be in line with our pricing on the Star line.

       Is there anything else we should discuss? Are you satisfied we've covered all of your concerns?

PM: I can't think of anything else.

VP: Are you sure this is what you want to do?

PM: Yes. I'm for turning the business over to you.

VP: (To buyer) Are you willing to release the order to us tomorrow?

Ann: Yes, I have some work to do first. I'll need the Purchasing Manager's signature on the first order because it's so large, and because we're depending on you for a critical delivery schedule.

VP: Will the Purchasing Manager be in tomorrow?

Ann: Good thought. Let me check right now.

The buyer leaves and returns in ten minutes.

Ann: The Purchasing Manager will be in tomorrow. I've

discussed everything with him and he'll be glad to sign off on your order since you're solving a big problem for us.

VP: Is there anything else we should know or discuss today about the packaging for the Sun line?

PM: No, I think that wraps it up. If you have any further questions give me a call. Thanks for your prompt attention.

VP: You're welcome. (PM leaves) (To Ann) Do you want to talk about packaging for your Moon line?

Ann: Not yet. We can discuss the Moon line after you show you can do as good a job with Sun as you have with Star. I don't want to take the chance of overloading you, and I still have a few months to deal with the Moon situation.

VP: Will we have the opportunity to work with you on Moon when the time is right?

Ann: Providing your performance remains good. We always look to our Favored Vendors first.

VP: I'll see you tomorrow with our quote.

Ann: Thanks, it's been a pleasure.

VP: You're welcome.

In the car on the way back to the office, the following conversation took place:

Sal: That deal will probably make them WPC's biggest customer. It sure was lucky you had an appointment with them today.

VP: Lucky?

Sal: Well, if we weren't there when the packaging problems came up, they might've given the business to someone else.

VP: What went on in that meeting wasn't luck. That packaging problem has been going on for some time, as you heard. My approach uncovered it and got it on the table. That's why I didn't want to tell you about High Probability Selling before you saw it for yourself. If you think about the entire sales call, you'll realize that very little of what went on was due to luck. Don't compare what you saw today with any of your old ideas about sales.

Sal: It seems to me that all you did was keep asking closing questions.

VP: That's just what I mean. Maybe that's only what you think you heard.

Sal: Well, because you've dealt with that buyer before, you already knew what was important to her. So you were able to handle her objections before she brought them up.

VP: So you noticed that she didn't raise a single objection. But that didn't happen for the reason you've suggested. She was too busy negotiating a solution to her problems to raise any objections. And consider also that because she wasn't pressured, there wasn't any resistance. What else do you think happened?

Sal: You closed on a minor point, when you asked the two

of them about delivery requirements.

VP: Maybe that's what it looked like, but I never asked about delivery dates. The Product Manager brought up delivery. I wasn't trying to close on a minor point.

Sal: Then what were you trying to do?

VP: I was trying to find out what their delivery requirements were.

Sal: Then I'm confused. I thought you were going to show me this great new, high-powered sales technique, and all you did was gather information.

VP: The human mind tends to fit everything into patterns and to group patterns into familiar categories. Most of the time that's helpful because it lets us apply our knowledge and experience to new situations, without thinking and planning about every little thing. But when it comes to learning something really new, like High Probability Selling, that approach is counterproductive. A really **new** idea doesn't fit into pre-existing patterns. The context is brand new.

The fact is you saw a powerful new sales technology this morning, and you didn't recognize it. Wait until tomorrow. When we go back with our quote and get their purchase order, you'll have real evidence of the effectiveness of High Probability Selling.

Sal: I really have no idea what you're talking about. I saw what happened today, and it looked like you handled the situation quite well. Maybe I'm even catching on to the fact that because it looked so easy, more like dumb luck than effective selling, that you did something I don't even understand. But, why did you demonstrate something to me that I couldn't understand?

VP: To open up your thinking. That's difficult for most people to do. Especially in an area you think you already know a lot about.

Sal: So, isn't it about time you explained some of this to me? Or should I watch you again with another customer?

VP: No. It's time to talk. As soon as we get back to the office, I'll go over the fundamentals of High Probability Selling with you.

CHAPTER THREE

High Probability Selling
& Traditional Selling:
A Comparison

VP: To begin with let's discuss two important differences between traditional selling and High Probability Selling.

First, traditional sales training teaches that just about everyone who might need what we sell is a prospect who can and should be sold. High Probability Selling takes a little sharper look at reality. There are clearly many more prospects out there than can ever be given our full sales and marketing message. If you try to sell every prospect, you'll waste time, money and effort. And, even more importantly, you'll waste the "opportunity cost" of not getting to those prospects who are most likely to buy, now.

Second, traditional sales training teaches that selling is the Art of Persuasion - that the way you get a prospect to buy your product or service is to manipulate the prospect through the five classical steps of the buying decision. In contrast, High Probability Selling teaches that selling is the art of Agreement and Commitment. Only High Probability Prospects - those who are willing to commit step-by-step to the buying process - are worth the salesperson's time, energy and resources.

Sal: But how can you tell whether someone is a High Probability Prospect before you've gone through a presentation?

VP: That's what you'll learn in High Probability Selling. The basic idea is to **disqualify** prospects who don't fit certain criteria, and that can happen at any point in the process.

Sal: If selling isn't persuading people to do what you want them to do, then what is it?

VP: Selling is reaching a series of agreements with those prospects who first acknowledge that they need, want and can afford what we're selling, and commit to buy from us at a specified time if we fulfill their Conditions of Satisfaction.

Sal: I was taught that you start by identifying a need, and then try to persuade the prospect that your product is what they want and that they can afford it. If you get that far, you go into your closing techniques, one by one. I was also taught that if customers say no often enough, they will eventually say yes, and that one yes is worth ten no's. So, until they get tired of saying no, you're supposed to keep on pitching.

VP: What most salespeople don't realize is they're wasting a lot of good selling opportunities by seeing too many of the wrong prospects. That wastes time, talent, energy, emotional strength and company resources.

Sal: Well, how do you know whether you have a good prospect until you try to sell him?

VP: Good question. It raises a lot of complex issues. We'll begin with some key points about prospects that most salespeople know but usually ignore. Here's how we categorize them:

1. Some prospects already need, want, and can afford what we sell. That group is happy to buy from us.

2. Some prospects need and can afford what we sell but do not want it.

3. Some prospects need and want what we sell but can't afford it.

4. Some prospects need, want and can afford what we sell, but won't buy from us. Like prospects who want what we sell, but prefer another brand or source.

Obviously we should be spending most of our time and resources talking to prospects in category one. The problem is those prospects don't wear a big red "one" on their foreheads. So, how do you recognize them?

Sal: You can't. Especially before they know whether they need and want what you're selling. And they can't know that until they hear your presentation. Which is why you try to sell every prospect you meet with.

VP: Not so. Most prospects make up their minds about an offer in the first minute. That's about all the time worth spending when you're prospecting. And what you're describing also requires the salesperson to be "aggressive" and "persistent."

Sal: Are you going to tell me that being aggressive and persistent doesn't work either?

VP: **Aggressive salespeople create defensive prospects. Persistence breeds annoyance.** Those approaches and other things salespeople do to manipulate prospects in order to get an appointment are what cause "sales resistance."

Sal: I don't get it. Are you saying that most of what I've learned over the years about selling doesn't work?

VP: Yes, and the hardest thing for you will be to give up those approaches, especially aggressiveness and persistence.

Sal: That's hard to believe. They're so much a part of selling that a lot of the help wanted ads for sales-people even advertise for those qualities.

VP: I know. But let me give you some background to help you understand.

The Traditional Sales Culture

Traditional Attributes of an All Star Salesperson:

A.	Ambitious	F.	Good Dresser
B.	Aggressive	G.	Charismatic
C.	Persistent	H.	Energetic
D.	Glib	I.	Fast Thinking
E.	Hard Driving		

Most companies would gladly accept this list, maybe adding a few more points of their own such as: tireless, holds his liquor, good golfer, etc. Although the world has changed quite a bit since this list was compiled, no one has taken the time to re-examine it.

Traditional sales techniques were developed on a psychological foundation that was largely misinterpreted. What they came up with was:

Attention	(The Sizzle)
Interest	(The Benefits)
Desire	(Need and Want)
Conviction	(Resolution of Doubt and Objections)
Action	(Close)

Millions of people were taught sales techniques based on this model despite the fact that most salespeople found them difficult to learn and uncomfortable to apply. Keep in mind that this technology was based on the idea that you could use psychology to **make** almost anyone buy almost anything.

That approach worked, or it seemed to for a while, because the most aggressive, most glib, and most ambitious people learned the system first and best. They were the people who sold a lot of storm windows, freezers, aluminum siding, and cars.

But a lot of buyers reacted with heavy-duty sales resistance. The problem was with the notion that people could be persuaded to buy a widget even if they didn't want one and that almost anyone could be trained to sell widgets. Many salespeople who tried that approach found that the failure and frustration were not worth the effort. Don't get me wrong! The basic psychology may be correct but the applications have been way off the mark.

Sal: Everybody knows someone who's a sales star. There's usually someone in every organization who's successful using traditional selling methods.

VP: Most successful salespeople don't know what it is about their style that works. They know and use many different approaches depending on the circumstances.

Instinctively they do whatever works to get the order. I've questioned a lot of successful salespeople about their work, and watched many of them in action. They all seem to have different ideas about what it is they do that works. But what they actually do is rarely the same as what they say they do.

Without trying to, most good salespeople ultimately develop very similar approaches. We've identified those approaches and examined them. We've discovered that what works is very different from what we were taught traditionally. And what we've learned fits into a pattern that is governed by certain basic principles, which is why High Probability Selling is called a technology.

Sal: How does High Probability Selling differ from what I've always done?

VP: First of all, traditional sales has a basic rule that "you should always ask for the order." In fact, some systems tell you to keep asking for the order until the prospect throws you out. **We never ask for the order.**

Sal: **That is different.** Everything I've ever been taught or read about selling says you always have to ask for the order. What else is different?

VP: Do you remember when we discussed spending your resources on prospects who need, want, and can afford what we sell? Well, the closer a prospect fits that description, the higher the probability he will buy from us. We don't waste time trying to sell prospects who probably won't buy from us. Why waste the effort? That's a basic shift in philosophy.

Sal: Well, if you're not trying to convince prospects to buy what you're selling, why do you need salespeople at all?

VP: That's a good question. The answer is contained in the question: "What's the role of the salesperson in the nineties?"

Back in the fifties it cost very little to have someone on the streets knocking on doors. Back then salespeople either worked on straight commission or received a small draw against commission. At very little cost companies had salespeople making calls on anyone and everyone. Of course, most salespeople didn't last very long under those conditions.

Television was available but it wasn't very sophisticated, and TV had almost no value as an informational medium. Only a small fraction of the news, trade and business magazines in circulation today existed then. Direct mail wasn't automated. So overall, there was much less advertising and publicity to educate and inform the market.

Salespeople were the "missionaries" who penetrated the market with new products and services. Their job was to convince as many prospects as possible that they needed, wanted and could afford these new widgets the salesperson was selling. But most industries can't afford missionaries any more.

Sal: Well, it's obvious that it's not cost effective to have salespeople do a company's advertising. But why isn't it cost effective to have salespeople out there trying to convince every logical prospect to buy from them?

VP: As a salesman, which would you prefer? Meeting with fifteen prospects, whom you **sold** on the idea of giving you an appointment (who each probably regretted giving you one as soon as they hung up); or seeing five High Probability Prospects, who've already told you that they need, want and can afford what you're selling and will buy from you now, if you can meet certain criteria?

Sal: Some choice. But how do you get appointments like that?

VP: For starters you have to eliminate sales resistance in the prospects you contact.

Sal: I've been taught that sales resistance shows up as "objections," so you have to either answer the objections before they're raised, or handle them as soon as they come up.

VP: We don't **handle** objections. In a High Probability Selling environment, the prospect is involved in the process of reaching agreement with you, not trying to resist being convinced. "Objections" don't surface as arguments or reasons why the prospect won't buy. They surface as points that have to be addressed, discussed and negotiated.

Sal: I think I'll just have to see that in action to understand it.

VP: I agree!   Here's more background. I'll give you a quick review of traditional selling techniques.

FIFTIES SALES TECHNOLOGY

Prospecting: The typical salesperson of the fifties started with a list of prospects that was "the market." Then the salesperson did whatever he had to do to get appointments with as many prospects as possible. He used any kind of scheme, strategy or trick available to get in the door. Once the salesperson came face to face with a prospect, he was told to hit them with everything, the full pitch, the whole "dog and pony show" - complete with "bells and whistles."

A "pitch" was usually a prepared presentation, complete with visual aids. It was usually modeled as a "five-step sales presentation," organized to follow the five psychological states a prospect goes through when buying. I mentioned them before but let's go over them in a little more detail.

1. *Attention*
Get the prospect's attention. Use showmanship, say something enticing, do whatever's necessary to get him to focus on what you're selling. The more dramatic, the better.

2. *Interest*
Hook the prospect with a strong emotional appeal connected to your product or service. Show the men the picture of the red convertible with the blonde in the passenger seat (notice that you can see her face, but you can't see the male driver's face - it might even be him). Show the women the picture of a woman in a neat station wagon, with happy children sitting quietly in their seat belts. It's "Show (business) Time." (The example for women would probably be much different today but the idea is the same.)

3. *Desire*
This is the seduction. Show them all the great features of your product or service and how it can benefit them. Give a great presentation, paint beautiful word-pictures. Get the prospect involved. Let them try it, taste it, or test drive it (if possible).

4. *Conviction*
Show them statistical proof of your product's superi-

ority. Use endorsements from prominent people who say they're delighted with your product or service. Or show them testimonial letters, certifications from customers, the government, their church, etc. All the while the salesman asks, "Wouldn't you like to?" questions and nods his head.

5. *Action (close)*

Test their reaction, ask for the order, handle their objections, and hit them with your favorite closing technique. There are hundreds of them. If they say no, find their objection. If it's hidden, dig it out. Handle the objection and close with a different technique. No sale? Do it again, and again, and again, with a little variation each time.

VP: As you can see, the whole approach is very manipulative and adversarial. It also takes a lot of time, a lot of energy and a ton of practice. It's also difficult to do without offending the prospect. And what's most offensive to prospects is that the salesperson does almost all of the talking. IN THIS PLAY THE CUSTOMER'S ONLY ROLE IS ANSWERING YES TO RHETORICAL QUESTIONS.

Sal: What's wrong with the five-step model - Attention, Interest, Desire, Conviction, and Action (Closing)?

VP: It may be accurate as a **buying** model. But as a **selling** model, it doesn't work. It's manipulative. When you use it as a selling model, you're trying to control the prospect by **leading** him through the steps. Being manipulated is insulting and annoying to people and leading a prospect through the five steps also takes a lot of time and effort.

Here are some of the basic problems with using the Five-Step Model when you sell:

Attention

If you have to do something unusual to get a prospect's attention, you don't have a very good prospect; certainly not a High Probability Prospect. Disqualifying a prospect like that prevents you from wasting your time. When you're offering people something they want, they naturally pay attention.

Interest

A lot of time is wasted trying to get uninterested people interested, and in boring people who are already interested. **More importantly, there are a lot of interested people who won't act. The prospect's level of interest is meaningless. What counts is whether your prospect wants what you have to sell.**

Desire

Rather than creating desire for your product or service by telling prospects about its features and benefits, you should be showing them how your product satisfies the desires they already have. But that should only be done after they've made a conditional commitment to buy.

Conviction

By the time you get to this step, you're in the "Can You Top This" mode. While you're showing, telling and proving, the prospect has yet to either set the limits for his satisfaction or make any commitment.

Action

If you don't close until the end of your presentation you've put out too much effort for an uncertain result. That invites crushing disappointment. In High Probability Selling the **entire process** is the close.

Sal: I know about the five-step sales approach, but never thought of it as being really effective. When I first learned it, I used it a lot but it felt awkward. After a while I just concentrated on my closing techniques, and with a lot of practice, I improved my closing rate.

VP: How much?

Sal: Well, I probably improved by 20 or 25 percent over a six month period. But it involved so much practice and concentration that after a while I just couldn't keep it up.

VP: Learning High Probability Selling requires effort as well, and lots of practice. But once you learn it, selling becomes easier and more natural and you'll increase your sales. And it's not a matter of concentration. Once you learn it, you own it. It becomes part of you.

Sal: You still haven't explained why the traditional five-step selling model is inaccurate.

VP: You misunderstood me. I said that it may be accurate as a buying model but not as a selling model. The technology that was developed to manipulate a prospect through the five steps in order to sell him isn't effective. If you want to sell as many prospects as you can within the time you have available, it's much more efficient to start with prospects who already want your product or service. With that in mind, we skip the first four steps and **begin** with the "Action" (close) step. That's where you want a prospect's attention. But, we don't use traditional closing techniques. We have too much respect for people to manipulate them. After you learn more about High Probability Prospecting, you'll see that we're always closing.

Sal: It still sounds like you're trying to get the prospect to do something you want him to do. Isn't that the same objective traditional selling has?

VP: No. High Probability Selling is a totally different approach. Traditional selling does try to get the prospect to do something, whether he wants to or not. Our object is to determine whether you and the prospect have a mutually beneficial basis for doing business, and if not, to go your separate ways. If there isn't mutual agreement and mutual commitment at any point in the discussion, the process stops. We continuously give the prospect every opportunity to disqualify himself, early and often, from beginning to end. As a result, if you and the prospect get through the three phases of the process, there's a very high level of assurance that both of you will get the result that you each want. The three phases of High Probability Selling are:

       High Probability Prospecting
       High Probability Selling
       High Probability Closing.

Sal: Sounds easy.

VP: The principles are easy to learn. The hard part is changing your old selling habits, like talking a blue streak trying to persuade people to do what **you** want them to do. Talk to our salespeople. They've all learned High Probability Selling. I think you'll decide that it's worthwhile to give up the struggle and save the effort and frustration.

Sal: It's worth a shot. But I think it's going to be hard to give up what I've worked so hard to learn.

CHAPTER FOUR

High Probability Selling Applied:
Some New Concepts

Over the next several days, as part of his training program, Sal went out on calls with two WPC salespeople, Sue and Larry. They had both worked for WPC before VP was brought in to "revitalize" the sales department. When VP first joined the company they were skeptical of his relaxed style. But after they saw him bring in several large new accounts, they decided to find out how he did it. What they saw was different, but so effective that they both learned High Probability Selling.

When Sal saw Sue and Larry in action he had no idea what was going on. Each had very different styles from the other and from VP. The only thing they all seemed to have in common was that they kept asking questions. Some of the questions seemed pointless, and others seemed intrusive. In fact, Sal often felt uncomfortable about some of the questions they asked.

On a call with Sue to meet a new prospect, after about ten minutes of questions and answers, Sue was asked for a quote on packaging. She answered saying that since the quote obviously wouldn't result in any business, she wasn't willing to have her sales estimating department prepare it. She courteously planted some seeds for possible future business, but instead of pressing forward, she made a quick exit.

Sal was surprised and after they left he asked Sue about what had gone on. When she told him that it would be more appropriate if VP explained it, he was more surprised.   He thought she wouldn't want VP to know what had happened.

Sal dropped the subject and asked Sue whether learning High Probability Selling had made a difference in her career.   She told him that her commissions had really taken off.   She emphasized she was more relaxed at work and felt better about herself, that she had more dignity and self-esteem, and that she was more in control of the selling process.

When they met again the next day, Sal asked VP about the call Sal had gone on with Sue.   VP explained she had done the right thing.   She had worked with the prospect only as long as he appeared to be a "HIGH PROBABILITY PROSPECT."   As soon as it became apparent that he was unlikely to be a customer then or in the near future, she courteously ended the visit.   She was correct in not using the company's resources in a no-win activity.   VP maintained that most prospects respect that kind of no-nonsense approach.

Sal said he didn't understand why the prospect didn't qualify as a High Probability Prospect.   In fact, he thought it was a positive sign that the prospect had asked for a quote.   VP pointed out that was not the case.   He said that based on what was said before the prospect requested the quote, Sue was clear either that we weren't getting any business in the near future or that the prospect was unresponsive or non-communicative. Most likely, it was the prospect's unwillingness to have a frank and open discussion that had Sue end the meeting when she did.

Sal: I think she had a lot of nerve asking some of the questions she asked.   It's no wonder he didn't answer them.

VP: Soon you'll see the value of those questions, and the value of **not going forward** when you don't get clear and honest answers to them.   This is a good time to tell you about some basic principles of High Probability Selling.

High Probability Selling is really **a method of inquiry**. The inquiry is designed to arrive at a meeting of the minds and result in mutual commitments between the salesperson and the prospect by determining whether:

A.   The prospect **needs, wants, and can afford** our product;

B.   The prospect is willing to define his **Conditions of Satisfaction** which, if met, will result in the purchase of our product; and,

C.   The **commitment** the prospect makes with regard to his Conditions of Satisfaction is specific as to all the necessary particulars and is absolute and unequivocal.

Sal: A few things make sense already. Sue cut the visit short right after she asked, "On what basis, if any, would you be willing to have us supply some of your packaging materials - as a second source supplier?" The prospect asked what she meant by that, and she said, "Would the right price, or fast delivery, or guaranteed top quality be a deciding factor?"

He said something like, "Just quote on our requirements and you'll find out whether you quoted right if you receive an order.   Our criteria for making those decisions are not your concern."   After a few more attempts to get that question answered, she ended the visit and we left.

VP: Sue was following a basic principle of High Probability Selling: **Don't waste your resources on Low**

Probability Prospects.

Sal: But as long as we were already there, she could've stayed and tried to do business with him.

VP: If she did that, she would've had to make a commitment for a quote. Then our estimating department would have to work up the quote, the department head would have to check it, and then we would have to generate a computer printout.

Sue would also have had to review the quote with the estimator, and return to the **Low Probability Prospect** to present the quote and sample materials. She probably would've had to make at least one follow-up call, too. The prospect might even ask her to revise the quote or bring back more samples, which would create another round of work. Even after all of that, the probability of actually getting an order would be low at best.

All that activity costs money. More importantly, it takes us away from the **opportunity** of working with High Probability Prospects. Also keep in mind that the intangible emotional drain on the salesperson of working with a low probability prospect is a hidden, but very considerable, additional cost.

Sal: What about all those questions the salespeople ask? It seems to me a lot of what they ask about is personal information a prospect would rather not discuss.

VP: You're probably right in a traditional sales situation. There the salesperson and the customer are adversaries. It's hard to have a sincere relationship with your enemy. In High Probability Selling the object is to build a relationship based on mutual trust and respect. In order to do that it's necessary to find out who the prospect really is. The **salesperson** gets ripped off with anything less.

Sal: Does that mean if the prospect isn't open and honest with us, we don't deal with him?

VP: Exactly.

Sal: Damn. That goes against all the training I've ever had. I was always taught to keep on talking and stressing benefits as long as a prospect will listen. And when he starts to nod his head or begins to say yes when I ask him positive questions, then it's time to close.

VP: High Probability Selling is very different. First, we clarify what it is the prospect wants, and we both agree on exactly what those wants are. We call those wants the prospect's **Conditions Of Satisfaction.** Second, assuming we can fulfill those Conditions Of Satisfaction profitably, we negotiate mutual commitments. In other words, we get crystal clear on what each of us promises to do. When you're negotiating commitments, you're into what you've always called the "close."

Sal: So, we're almost always asking instead of telling.

VP: Right. You should frame most of what you have to say in the form of a question. The prospect should do most of the talking, primarily answering your questions. The more the prospect talks, the more both of you win.

Sal: But if you don't tell the prospect about the company's capabilities, and why our products and services are better than the competition's, how will he know?

VP: The more you try to convince the prospect that your product is the best, the more resistance you create.

Understand this, almost anything you say can be phrased as a question. As long as you're asking questions, the prospect remains involved in the conversation. Let me give you some examples:

You ask: Do you prefer to have your packages shipped open or flat with one push to open?

Prospect: Does WPC ship them flat?

You ask: Yes, is that what you want?

You ask: Are you willing to pay more for top quality and on time deliveries?

Prospect: Yes. We might have to shut down a production line if the quality of the packaging is off. And on time delivery is especially important to us because we've recently gone to just-in-time deliveries and we don't keep back-up supplies of inventory.

You ask: What else do you want?

VP: Whether the customer prefers flat packages or is willing to pay more for top quality and timely deliveries, he's likely to talk about the choices. A prospect may have good reasons for not wanting our products. His product may lend itself better to open packaging. Or low price may be his highest priority. In any case, you save a lot of time by learning those things before you spend time and resources on him. Also, when you're focusing on what **the prospect** has to say, your ideas on how to serve **him** are welcomed, especially when those ideas are phrased as questions.

Sal: I still don't understand how and when you close.

VP: That's okay for now. Go over the examples we just discussed. There were probably a number of what you would consider "closing questions."

Sal: Maybe, but gathering information isn't closing.

VP: The entire High Probability Selling process is a closing process. You probably noticed when you went on sales calls last week that when we asked questions and got answers that justified going on, we asked for commitments. We ask questions like: "Is that what you want?" or "Is there anything else we should cover?" or "Are you willing to pay a ten per cent premium for a glossy finish?" or "If we show you we can meet your requirements, what will you do?"

Sal: That doesn't make sense to me. When do you ask for the order?

VP: WE NEVER ASK FOR THE ORDER!

Sal: (Incredulous) Well, do you use closing techniques at all?

VP: As I said before the entire High Probability Selling process is a closing process. We focus on finding out what's necessary to do business, right from the start. We use an orderly process that's thorough and professional. Our approach is designed to have the prospect commit to do business with us if what we have is what he wants.

Sal: Suppose the customer doesn't do that?

VP: In that case we did something wrong. Maybe we didn't disqualify the prospect when we should have. Perhaps we moved to a new phase without a **commitment.** When we reach a point where a prospect won't make commitments, we end the meeting and move on to someone else.

The fault however, if there is one, is ours. We may not have qualified the prospect correctly, or maybe some old fashioned "power selling" snuck through by accident and created resistance. **BUT NEVER ASK FOR THE ORDER!** Just negotiate mutual commitments. In a situation where our company can't fulfill the prospect's Conditions of Satisfaction, acknowledge that promptly and make a swift, courteous exit.

Sal: Do you mean like when he needs a type of material that we don't supply?

VP: That's a good example. Another is when the prospect wants fast deliveries and low price. As you know, we can give him fast deliveries and top quality, but the price has to reflect that.

Sal: How do you convince him that he should want fast deliveries and top quality at a higher price?

VP: You don't ever try to convince a prospect that he needs and wants what you have to sell. If he clearly understands the benefits you're offering, and they're not what he wants, it's time to end that visit. If he really wants what you have, he won't let you go.

Sal: Doesn't that require a strong presentation?

VP: No. But it requires the right questions, such as:

You said you wanted a fast cycle time, how fast?

You said you wanted the most insurance you could buy for a $1,500 annual premium. Do you want me to shop the market for you or are you planning to do your own shopping, company evaluation and comparison analysis?

You said you want the fastest possible delivery. Are you willing to pay a premium for the overtime necessary to fill that requirement?

Sal: Well, that's like asking the kind of "closing questions" they teach in a lot of sales courses.

VP: Not so. Most prospects have heard enough "closing questions" to know exactly what you're doing, and resent it. We're sincere in trying to determine the prospect's Conditions of Satisfaction (and we tell him what we're doing when we're doing it) and he can sense the difference.

Sal: How is what you're asking different than closing on a minor point, such as: "Do you want the blue or the grey?" or "Do you prefer deliveries on Tuesday or Thursday?"

VP: In High Probability Selling we don't ask rhetorical or manipulative questions. We only ask questions we need to know the answers to.

Sal: If you're only asking questions, how do you convince the prospect that he needs and wants your product?

VP: Do you remember the first call you went on with me?

Sal: Yes.

VP: As I recall, you thought it was just "dumb luck" that they gave me their business.

Sal: Now I remember. I was wondering how you could just sit there and ask them what they wanted to do, when all of that business was there for the asking.

VP: Do you also remember how reluctant Ann was to talk to me about any business except for the Star product line which we already handle?

Sal: Yes. But once she started talking about the bind she was in, you could've asked her for the order.

VP: At that point she hadn't made any commitments to change vendors. In fact, the discussion started as a complaint. It was only because I asked questions, gave her choices and asked for commitments, that we received that order. And, as you know, their requirements for the Sun line are about three times greater than for the Star line.

Sal: But why did you wait for them to offer you the business? Why didn't you just ask for an order?

VP: There were several reasons. First, as you now know we never ask for the order. Second, when I asked what they needed and wanted, **they** defined their Conditions of Satisfaction. If I had asked for a commitment to buy at that point, and been unable to meet their Conditions of Satisfaction, the order would've been jeopardized. If you're not able to satisfy some of their Conditions of Satisfaction, you negotiate those conditions. If you can work them out, then you ask for a commitment. That's what happened when the Product Manager agreed to have us redo the art work just for the first four packages, rather than doing them all at once.

If you create an environment where the prospect is the one doing the talking, he's more likely to open up and tell you exactly what he wants, actually lay out for you all his Conditions of Satisfaction. You don't have to convince anyone of anything, or guess at what they want to hear, or even handle objections.

Sal: Then why did you **keep** asking everyone **whether they were sure that was what they wanted to do**? I was sure you would lose the order when you kept doing that.

VP: Prospects usually have what you call "hidden objections" or second thoughts. It's better to get those thoughts out in the open while you're still there rather than have them surface after you leave. Also, by having the prospect assure you he's doing what **he** wants to do, **he** takes complete responsibility for giving you his business. Later on, he won't feel like he's been talked into anything, and he hasn't.

Sal: I have to admit I was surprised at how appreciative the customers were. That's not what I'm used to hearing.

VP: I know. That doesn't usually happen when you hammer people for an order, even if you eventually get it.

VP summarized what he called:

THE KEYS TO HIGH PROBABILITY SELLING

KEY: *End The Meeting If You Are Unable To Complete Any Phase Of The Process.*
Rather than trying to transform a Low Probability Prospect into a High Probability Prospect, your time is better spent talking with someone who already is a High Probability Prospect.

KEY: *The Inquiry Method.*

In order to move forward through the High Probability Process, you and your prospect must have a **meeting of the minds.** You already know what you have to offer, but what does the prospect want? The quickest and most effective way to find out is by asking.

KEY: *Being Thorough At The First Meeting.*

Most people will answer almost any question you ask, truthfully and completely, provided you're not being manipulative and they sense that you really want to know the answers. When I say "sense" I mean the intuitive feeling you get about something or someone, a reaction that just comes to you without any thought. If your approach is really an honest one, deep down, the person you're talking with can sense it. So your questions have to be sincere and not threatening in any way. A first meeting only happens one time so it's important to ask everything you need to know, or might need to know in the future.

KEY: *Taking Notes.*

Taking complete notes is very important, because if you forget the prospect's answers, it may be difficult to get that information again. It's also embarrassing to forget what you've already been told and having to ask the same question again. Forgetting can cost you an account.

At every call be sure to have a substantial notebook, writing tablet, or questionnaire with you. Take it out at the beginning of the meeting and start writing. Write down everything of fact or opinion that the prospect says that relates to him or his business, and record it accurately. Three months later you may not be able to fill in the blanks.

Taking notes accomplishes two things. First, it shows the prospect that you really mean business and that you value what he has to say. Second, your notes provide information in its most useful form, the prospect's exact words. Those words will be invaluable when you establish his "Conditions of Satisfaction."

KEY: *Listening*.

When we ask questions, we do so for a reason. The purpose is to **learn something** the prospect knows and we don't. If you ask but don't listen, you defeat the purpose of your question. Listening is not easy, except when you're interested. Then listening is very easy. If you don't completely understand an answer or the prospect doesn't fully answer the question, ask another question to clarify things for you (and sometimes for the prospect). The more thoroughly the prospect answers our questions, the better our chances are of learning exactly what it will take to do business with him. At the same time we begin to get an idea of the probability of satisfying his criteria for buying and the probability of getting his business.

Don't think about your next question when the prospect is talking. Thinking comes after listening. If you don't listen, there will be little to say in response to what he's said. If you're not interested enough to listen attentively to what your prospect is saying, he'll sense that and he'll disqualify you. Focus on your conversation.

KEY: *Not Talking.*

Whenever the salesperson is talking, the prospect has a natural tendency to feel **pressured**. The pressure usually generates questions, statements, and all sorts of objections to what is being said to him. He gets the feeling you think what you have to say is more important than what he has to say. Since he's the prospect, what he has to say is more important than what you have to say. Button your lip.

If the salesperson is doing more than 25 percent of the talking, that's an indication that the meeting is not going well. At that point we ask ourselves why the prospect is non-responsive or why we're talking so much. If we can't rectify the problem, we should end the meeting unless we have a very strong indication that the prospect is just naturally on the quiet side - taciturn. But in most cases, a non-responsive prospect is a Low Probability Prospect.

KEY: *Never Respond To Anger; Defuse It or Leave.*
When faced with a prospect or customer who is angry, sarcastic, depressed, threatening, abusive or negative in any way, deal with that before you proceed with anything. Doing that successfully requires a good deal of self-control and the willingness to sublimate your own emotions.

Your approach to this kind of sensitive situation has to be voiced in a flat, non-emotional tone. You can't be either judgmental or sympathetic. You must be neutral. Use the same tone of voice you would use saying, "It looks like it might rain."

Step 1: "You seem upset."
Most often the response will be a heated explanation of why he's upset. Usually that begins with "You're darned right I'm upset." So far nothing has changed and he may be even more upset.

Step 2: "You still seem upset."
You must say this in a flat tone of voice with no emphasis on the word "still." He may start to calm down or he may still be upset.

Step 3: "Maybe we should discuss this at another time."
At this point the prospect will most often say that he's fine even if he isn't.

Step 4: Continue a dialogue as long as he remains calm. If he seems to get upset again, start over at Step 1. Be sure to stay flat and unemotional. If all else fails, go to step 5.

Step 5:   "I'm not willing to meet with you now. For us to meet now wouldn't serve you or me. Would you like to schedule another appointment, or not?"

Sal: Both of the salespeople I went out with last week did those things. I just figured they had a low-keyed style, operating that way; asking questions, taking notes, not saying much and letting the prospect do the talking. In fact, it looked like they weren't very persuasive or dynamic at all. They really seemed too laid back. Now I see that what I thought was "laid back" is really part of High Probability Selling.

VP: Good! By the way, how did they do?

Sal: They walked away with orders I thought they had no chance to get, even when the customers said they weren't interested. But doesn't talking with customers who aren't interested go against the rule of not wasting time with Low Probability Prospects?

VP: Good question.   It shows that you're starting to understand where we're coming from. The answer to your question points out one of the subtle aspects of High Probability Selling.

KEY: *Don't Respond To Non Sequiturs.*
You see, the statement, "I'm not interested" is a non sequitur. A non sequitur is an answer that follows a question but really doesn't answer it. The sequence doesn't make sense. In sales, a prospect often answers with a non sequitur as a defense mechanism.

Sal: Don't I have to say something when the customer says he's not interested?

VP: No. The prospect really hasn't asked you anything or said anything that calls for an answer. It's as if all he did was clear his throat or cough. What he said is just noise.

Sal: But I thought you end the meeting when the prospect gets negative.

VP: Another subtle distinction. Making noises, even if they sound like negative noises, doesn't disqualify a prospect.

Sal: You'll have to explain that.

VP: Well, suppose you ask a prospect whether he's the person responsible for choosing the vendor for their packaging materials, and he says, "I'm not interested in any new vendors." He didn't answer your question.

Sal: Maybe he didn't answer my question, but I sure can't ignore what he said.

VP: Yes, you can; you can treat it like a noise and ask for clarification. You can ask, "Mr. Prospect, does that mean selecting vendors for packaging materials **is** your responsibility, or does someone else handle that?"

Sal: Suppose he says that he **is** the one who makes that decision and that he's not interested in a new one.

VP: You go on treating the non sequitur part of what he says as noise. You can say something like, "Mr. Prospect, most of our customers don't use any more than two vendors for each product line. Is that how you operate too?"

Sal: Now I get it. As long as the prospect is answering your questions, you don't have to worry about the other stuff he says.

VP: You're starting to catch on. If he stays in the dialogue and answers your questions, there's a good chance he'll give up his resistance somewhere along the way. If, on the other hand, he makes it clear that he doesn't need or want what you're selling, or that he really can't afford it, don't ignore that. You may have a bona fide **Low Probability Prospect** on your hands.

Sal: How else do I recognize a Low Probability Prospect?

VP: Enthusiasm. A High Probability Prospect is usually responsive and enthusiastic about what you're offering. A Low Probability Prospect isn't.

Sal: When will I be able to try some of this with some live prospects?

VP: First, you'll need some prospects to call on. So, you'll need some practice in High Probability Prospecting before you get started. We can kill two birds with one stone by having you prospect on the phone for a few days. Tomorrow you can start training with Sue.

CHAPTER FIVE

High Probability Prospecting

The next day Sal began prospecting training with Sue. Sal hated prospecting with a passion. In his experience it was tedious, frustrating and generally depressing. Just thinking about prospecting brought up the old gut wrenching feelings.

By the time he met Sue at the office Sal was already anticipating a grueling, unpleasant day. Sue told him to get a cup of coffee and relax while she cleaned up her desk. He waited while she went through her mail and prepared several quotation requests for the estimating department. To Sal, it seemed that Sue was trying to avoid getting started for as long as she could, which, as far as he was concerned, was understandable. When Sue finished what she was doing she picked up a list and called the first company.

Sue: Hello, this is Sue Green from WPC Packaging. I need your help. (pause) Who's the person in your company responsible for packaging design? (pause) Okay, how does your marketing manager spell his last name? (pause) Oh, Jackson, what's his first name? Thank you. Is he available now? (pause) Thanks for your help. (pause) Hello, this is Sue Green of WPC Packaging. To whom am I speaking? Hello, Dolores. I need your help. I'm not sure whether I should speak with Bob Jackson or with someone else in your company. Is Bob Jackson responsible for your company's product packaging? (pause) Oh, each product has a product manager who handles packaging for his own line. What are their names? (pause) That's Mike Starns and Jerry

Sikouski? Thank you very much for your help. I'll stop by and say hello when I visit your company. Bye now. (Hang up)

Sal: Why did you ask for the Marketing Manager?

Sue: In a lot of firms receptionists are told not to give out any names but the marketing and sales manager's. If you're having a problem reaching them, you can always get to talk to someone in the sales department.

Sal: That seemed pretty easy. But why didn't you try to talk to Bob Jackson? You already had his secretary on the line.

Sue: Because it's foolish to waste time talking to the wrong person.

Sal: But you know that eventually the marketing manager is going to get involved in any packaging changes.

Sue: That's probably true. But if Jackson is part of the decision-making process, I'll get him involved soon enough. My first priority is to get to the person who has the primary responsibility for making a decision on our products.

Sal: But you could've gotten some important background information on the company by talking to the marketing manager - like their marketing philosophy or information about their product lines.

Sue: There's no need to learn those things now. First I have to find out whether they're a High Probability Prospect.

Sal: Well, are you going to call the product managers? Or are you going to send them brochures and samples first?

Sue: I'll call them in a minute. As far as sending them something is concerned, we usually don't send out unsolicited mail. We limit unsolicited mailings to our mass mailings, which we send out two or three times a year.

A couple of minutes later Sue called Mike Starns, one of the three product managers.

Sue: Hello, Mike, this is Sue Green from WPC Packaging. We manufacture self-contained, four-color display packaging, which is shipped flat and is easy to assemble. Is that something you want for your product line? (pause) Does that mean that you aren't ready to make any changes **now**, or that you don't plan to make any changes later, as well?... because if you don't want me to call back, that's okay...just say so. (pause) Sure, I'll call back in about three weeks. Will that be to set up an appointment or what? (pause) Okay, and when we meet what should we aim to accomplish? (pause) Okay, then I'll bring a few samples of that type of material, so that we'll be in a position to agree on a sample order. Let's set a tentative date for three weeks from today and I'll call to confirm the day before. Is that okay? (pause) What time is good for you? (pause) Nine is fine for me. Should Bob Jackson be available? (pause) Okay, I'll see you then. Bye now.

Sal: How can you say that?

Sue: Say what?

Sal: How can you tell him it's okay if he doesn't want you to call him back?

Sue: Because it is. I don't want to waste my time with anyone who doesn't want what I'm selling or doesn't want to talk to me.

Sal: Well, you're lucky he's looking to make some packaging changes now.

Sue: Luck had nothing to do with it. He had an idea in the back of his mind that he might need something new and he realized from my approach that I wasn't going to spend a lot of time pursuing him. He was on the spot. So, he decided to take the opportunity to meet with me. When you're straight with people about your needs, they're much more likely to be straight with you. And it saves a whole lot of wasted time and effort.

Sal: Talking about a sample order with a buyer you've never met was pretty pushy.

Sue: That wasn't "pushy." I was direct and honest and he knew it. The truth works as well in business situations as it does anywhere else. Besides, I don't get paid for making social calls.

Sue then called the other product manager, Jerry Sikouski, but Sikouski wasn't in. So she made a call to another company.

Sue: Hello, Ray Jefferies please. (pause) Hello, Ray. This is Sue Green from WPC Packaging. We spoke six weeks ago and you suggested that I get back to you this week to see whether you had budget approval for a packaging change. You said if you were able to get budget approval, you might want to switch to self-contained, four-color display packaging, which is shipped flat and is easy to assemble. (pause) Does that mean you plan to stick with your current packaging permanently, or do you want me to check back with you in the future? (pause) No, okay. Is there anyone else in your company who I should speak with about packaging, maybe for one of your company's other lines? (pause) No, okay. Should we keep you on our mailing list? (pause) Okay, if we have any new developments that fit your needs I'll give you a call. Good bye.

Sal: Why didn't you tell him we have products that fit his needs right now?

Sue: Because he's not open to conversation now. And I'm not willing to spend any time trying to make him into something he's not.

Sal: What do you mean?

Sue: He's not a High Probability Prospect!

Sue then called the next name on her list.

Sue: Hello, Mr. Garson? Hi, this is Sue Green from WPC Packaging (pause) Oh, I understand that you're busy...do you want me to call back at another time? (pause) Mr. Garson, it's okay if you don't want to talk to me. Just say so, and I won't call again. (pause) Oh, I see....after your vacation. When do you get back? (pause) Wednesday....suppose I call you the following Monday morning. We can set up an appointment then. (pause) Okay, bye now.

Sal: Wow! You are tough. You didn't even wince when you told him it was okay to say he didn't want to talk to you. What would you have done if he told you not to call back?

Sue: What do you think? I would have done what he wanted. Later, I might have someone else give him a call.

Sal: Well, you practically invited him to kiss you off.

Sue: No, the invitation was direct. If the man doesn't want to do business with me, I'm better off knowing that before I spend any time on him.

Sal: Well, if he had told you not to call him back, why would you have had someone else call him later?

Sue: Because **he hadn't dis-qualified himself yet**.

Sal: Why not? What does a prospect have to do to get dis-qualified?

Sue: He has to indicate that he's not ready, willing and able to buy what we're selling.

Sal: I guess it's easy to be relaxed when you're the one who's doing the qualifying.

Sue: You've got things backwards. I'm the one who does the **dis-qualifying**. The prospect is the one who does the qualifying with his answers to my questions. And I only want straight answers. I don't trick prospects into making appointments. In some sales training courses they teach you to "sell the appointment." Don't do that. You only want to meet with fully qualified, High Probability Prospects.

Sal: When you talk about not wasting your time with Low Probability Prospects, are you saying that there are plenty of High Probability Prospects?

Sue: Yes, I am. There are lots of prospects out there. More than our entire sales staff could visit in three years. But, at any given time, the number of **High Probability Prospects** is usually small. Part of our job is to

identify them. That means contacting as many prospects as you can, as briefly as possible, with the intention of **identifying** the High Probability Prospects. And spending your time only with those prospects. The others are all disqualified.

Here's some more information to help you understand what I'm talking about:

The Dis-Qualification Process

Prospecting: The objective is to spend our selling time only with prospects who need, want and can afford our product, who are ready to buy **now** and are willing to buy from us. Keep in mind that we don't even want to make an appointment with anyone, unless he indicates he needs and wants what we have to offer. If he does, he'll be anxious to meet with us. We don't try to sell the appointment. During the phone call every effort is made to give the prospect the opportunity to **dis-qualify** himself. So, of course, the process is called, "Dis-Qualification."

Get all of the following information from the prospect before the appointment:

Does he want our product?
Does he want to arrange an appointment?
If not now, when?
If not now, does he want us to check back later?
Why does he want to meet with us at this time?
What would he like to accomplish at our meeting ?

There are other dis-qualification questions that fit particular circumstances. As salespeople make more and more prospecting calls, they become increasingly adept at asking **effective** questions and are able to quickly dis-qualify Low Probability Prospects. Ironically, prospects often attempt to qualify themselves and demand an appointment.

Sal: When you ask "Low Probability Prospects" whether they want you to call back, why do you add, "What is it you would like to accomplish by meeting with me?"

Sue: Just because someone starts off as a Low Probability Prospect, doesn't mean they'll always be in that category. You have to give them a chance to choose whether they want to qualify in the future.

Sal: But if it seems like the prospect will be a "High Probability Prospect" in the future, doesn't it make sense to get to know him and start to develop a relationship with him now?

Sue: What makes you think a prospect would be receptive to spending time with me when there's no urgency to buy what I'm offering?

Sal: I just think it's a good strategy.

Sue: If a prospect expresses a real desire to see me, and I think there's a reasonable chance business will result from a visit, now or in the near future, I would probably be willing to meet with him. But he would have to be very definite about it.

Sal: What do you gain by playing hard to get?

Sue: I'm not playing. I'm not willing to spend time with prospects who aren't willing to make commitments.

Sal: V.P. uses that word a lot. What do you mean by **commitments**?

Sue: Commitments are the central theme of High Probability Selling. We only commit our resources to people who make commitments to us. I'm sure that VP will cover that with you later in more detail. All of our salespeople commit to and require commitments from our prospects. That's what High Probability Selling is all about - trading commitments.

Sal: Tell me more about that.

Sue: I can't right now. Ask VP when you meet with him this afternoon. My assignment is to **show** you how I prospect, not tell you what to do.

Sue dialed another number.

Sue: Hello, Mr. Landi, this is Sue Green from WPC Packaging. We manufacture self-contained, four-color display packaging, which is shipped flat and is easy to assemble. Is that something you want for your product line? (pause) Does that mean that you're familiar with our product, or that you're not? (pause) Okay, good bye.

Sal: What happened? That call only took about ten seconds.

Sue: He said, "It was none of my business what he was familiar with." He disqualified himself right away by not being willing to talk.

Sal: But maybe you could've said something that would've gotten him interested.

Sue: Maybe. But I'm not willing to waste my time trying to persuade a six of clubs that he's really an ace of hearts. So I disqualified him quickly.

Sal: What do you mean by, "trying to persuade a six that it's an ace?"

Sue: Well, suppose I give you a deck of cards, face down, and tell you I'll give you five dollars for every ace you find in the next two minutes. And suppose the first card you turn up is a six. How much time would you spend trying to convince the six that it's an ace?

Sal: Well, like most analogies, that one's flawed. There've been times I **have** persuaded people who said they didn't need my product, that they really did; and they eventually bought from me.

Sue: That's why casinos make so much money from slot machines. If it weren't for the occasional reward, people wouldn't keep throwing their money into them. But if you know anything about the slots, you know that if you play them long enough you have to go broke. They're programmed that way.

Sal: So, what you're saying is that trying to "sell the appointment" is generally a losing proposition.

Sue: Unless you're getting paid for the number of appointments you make, whether you sell anything or not, "selling the appointment" is a flat-out losing approach.

Sal: But what about all those things I learned about "relationship building" and "a good first impression" and "determining personality type."

Sue: Good ideas if you're running for senator but a waste of time when prospecting. The point of High Probability Prospecting is that you meet **only** with people who qualify as High Probability Prospects.

Sal: That almost sounds too easy. There's no struggle left if you're not trying to get everyone to listen to what you have to say.

Sue: That's the intention.

Sal: And if they say no, there's no sense of rejection or failure since you're not trying to convince them to meet with you. You're only trying to **identify** High Probability Prospects.

Sue: That's right. There's plenty of rejection when you're selling, but no rejection when you're identifying.

After several calls in which Sue was unable to reach the person she was calling, she got through to Jack Magnum.

Sue: Hello, Mr. Magnum, this is Sue Green from WPC Packaging. We manufacture self-contained, four-color display packaging, which is shipped flat and is easy to assemble. Is that something you want for your product line? (pause) Is this type of packaging something that you want for your line, or not? (pause) Yes, it's more expensive than plain, corrugated cardboard. Are you willing to pay more for improved point of sale appearance? (pause) Do you want to meet to see if you can reduce your handling, assembly and storage costs, by using WPC packaging? (pause) If our packaging meets your criteria, what will you do? (pause) In that case, when do you want to meet? (pause) I'm busy Tuesday at 10:30. Can we make it Tuesday afternoon? Okay, I'll see you then. Bye now.

Sal: Wow! Talk about going for commitments. I can't believe you actually asked a prospect you've never met, who hasn't even seen our products yet, what he'll do?

Sue: Why? Remember what I told you about commitments.
         I'm not willing to meet with someone unless I have a
         commitment that we'll do business if our packaging
         meets his criteria.

Sue made several more calls and didn't get through to the
person she was calling. Her next call was to Susan Kaplan.

Sue: Hello, Mrs. Kaplan, this is Sue Green from WPC
         Packaging. We manufacture self-contained, four-color
         display packaging, which is shipped flat and is easy to
         assemble. Is that something you want for your product
         line? (pause)   Does that mean you do want self-
         contained, four-color display packaging, which is
         shipped flat and is easy to assemble, or not? (pause)
         Assuming those things can be worked out, is this type
         of packaging something you want or not? (pause) Are
         you sure? (pause) Do you want to meet to see if what
         we have is what you want? (pause) If our packaging
         meets your criteria, what will you do? (pause) When do
         you want to get together? (pause) Wednesday morning
         at nine is fine. See you then. Bye now.

Sal: That "or not" sounds harsh. I wince every time you
         say, "Is this something you want, **or not**?"

Sue: It doesn't sound harsh to the prospect. In fact, it makes
         it easier for the prospect to say yes, if that's what he
         wants to do. When you give the prospect the choice to
         say no, you're eliminating resistance and **requiring** the
         prospect to be responsible for his continued
         participation. When people know you're willing to take
         "no" for an answer, they're usually willing to talk with
         you, openly and honestly. You can't trust your intuition
         here. Your intuition may tell you that adding the "or
         not" is negative and confrontational, and may increase
         the chances of getting a "no." In actuality the opposite

is true.

Sal: Why did you keep asking Mrs. Kaplan whether she wanted our packaging? It sounded like she wanted more information and you wouldn't give it to her.

Sue: She was asking me about price and delivery terms. I don't discuss those issues unless I know the prospect wants what we're selling. Always find out whether the prospect wants what you're selling, subject to those other issues being worked out, before you go on.

Sal: What if the prospect can't determine whether she wants what we're selling unless certain questions are answered?

Sue: Then you answer those questions. But usually, if you say, "Assuming we can work those things out, is this something you want, or not?" the need to have those questions answered at that moment is eliminated.

Sal: Why do you say your opening line the same way each time?

Sue: You mean, "Hello, Mr. Prospect, this is Sue Green from WPC Packaging. We manufacture self-contained, four-color display packaging, which is shipped flat and is easy to assemble. Is that something you want for your product line?"

Sal: Yes, why do you say it like that?

Sue: The idea is to quickly paint a word picture that clearly describes what you have to offer. We call that "languaging your offer." It took me three rounds of trial prospecting calls to get my offer clear and concise. I've sharpened it a little since then based on some of the responses I've gotten from prospects. Now I've got it down to thirty-four words. The shorter the offer, the better the results.

Sal: I wouldn't word it the same way.

Sue: No problem. Your offer has to be in your own words and it has to make sense to you. You'll find out soon enough whether your language works. If prospects don't understand what you're saying, or seem resistant, you have to relanguage your offer. Most new people tend to make their offer too long. Try to keep yours under forty-five words. After you use it for a while you'll get a feel for what works.

Sal: Why do you always use the same tone of voice when you're speaking with prospects?

Sue: Words aren't the only things that can cause resistance. A "convincing" tone of voice can, too. It's important to language your offer in a neutral, unemotional tone of voice. In fact, when you're prospecting, everything you say should be in a neutral, unemotional tone. Anything you add can cause resistance. Keep it clean and simple.

Sal: Well, it's almost lunch time. How about a sandwich? I'm buying.

Sue: Thanks, but I can't. I have a meeting with a customer in a little while to show the product and get a purchase order.

Sal: Oh, you mean you're going to show him the product and then get a commitment.

Sue: No. I've already gotten a commitment.

Sal: How can you have a commitment when you haven't shown the product yet?

Sue: In High Probability Selling, we only demonstrate the product after the customer has made a commitment to buy, provided what we show him meets his criteria. What I'm telling you will only confuse you now. I'm sure that VP will clear that up for you. It's really much easier than it sounds. For now, just concentrate on the fundamentals of High Probability Prospecting.

 ## THE FUNDAMENTALS OF HIGH PROBABILITY PROSPECTING

1. **Clearly language your offer in 45 words or less, including your salutation and introduction.**

2. **Ask the prospect if he wants what you are offering.**

3. **If he answers yes, ask him if he wants to arrange a meeting with the intention of doing business; or**

4. **Reschedule your call to a time when the prospect wants you to contact him again, with his commitment to move forward at that time.**

5. **End the call if you get a negative answer to <u>any</u> of your questions. Schedule a call-back only if the prospect indicates he will be a High Probability Prospect at a specific future time. Assure the prospect that it is <u>okay to say "No"</u> whenever you sense hesitation on his part.**

6. **Dis-qualify every prospect who doesn't want what you're offering, or isn't willing to buy it from you.**

After lunch Sal went back to VP's office.

VP: What did you learn by watching Sue do her prospecting?

Sal: I learned a lot. It looked like she started with a lot of hot leads.

VP: Why do you say that?

Sal: Well, she didn't seem to get much resistance. In fact, most of the people she talked to were interested. She certainly got a lot of appointments for the time she spent. Seems she must have been working from a pretty good list.

VP: Sue was using an unscreened list of companies taken right out of a few trade directories.

Sal: That's hard to believe. Almost all the prospects responded as if they had already been screened.

VP: Now you see the power of the dis-qualification process. When you control the process and the prospect has to qualify, the results pretty much follow what you saw.

Sal: Why is that?

VP: When a prospect realizes you're not trying to "sell him on an appointment," he doesn't generate his usual sales resistance. And when a High Probability prospect senses you're politely trying to **dis-qualify him**, he'll naturally try to qualify himself.

Sal: That's the old "reverse psychology."

VP: I don't know what it is, but it's not a ploy. I **can** tell you that what we do is a lot more efficient than the old "sell the appointment" routine. **High Probability Prospecting is an identification process, not a selling process.** By the time you meet with a prospect, you know you're dealing with someone who needs what you're selling and wants to buy.

Sal: I was taught to conceal what I was selling when I prospected, and within limits, to say whatever I had to say to get the appointment.

VP: High Probability Prospects are especially careful because they **want** to buy. As a result, they're reluctant to admit their buying intention to someone they don't trust. Prospects are as perceptive as salespeople. If you're being evasive, or using deceptive prospecting tactics, they know it and don't trust you. If you state your offer clearly and concisely, and give them a choice, without any convincing, persuading or manipulation, prospects will usually take a minute to see whether they want what you're offering, instead of resisting you by reflex. When you try to convince and persuade, people resist - usually unconsciously - which often looks like hostility and evasiveness.

Sal: I wish I could just relax and feel comfortable with prospecting, like Sue.

VP: Be patient. It doesn't take very long. Start with your offer. Use language that allows you to clearly and concisely describe what you're selling.

Sal: I don't know if I can be comfortable saying some of the things Sue says.

VP: Don't worry about that. You don't have to say what she says. And don't get hung up about feeling comfortable. No one feels comfortable in a new environment. People even feel uncomfortable for a while in a new home. Comfort comes when you live in it for a while. When Sue was learning High Probability Prospecting, she was very uncomfortable. And she was uncomfortable when she was learning all the other stages of High Probability Selling, too.

Sal: Well, I don't do well when I feel uncomfortable.

VP: Welcome to the world. No one does. When you're learning, it's natural to feel uncomfortable, especially in sales. That's because you have to practice with live prospects, and everyone wants to look good in front of someone else. Since you know in advance that you probably won't look polished until you've tried it many times, you'll be anxious. That's natural, and there's no way to avoid it. During your first few calls, forget about doing it well. I'm your boss and I'll forget about that too. What's important for both of us is that you practice. The sales will come.

Sal: I hope so.

VP: You sound doubtful. What is it you're concerned about?

Sal: Everything I've seen you do is different from everything I was ever taught, and different from everything I've ever read about sales.

VP: Well, since you weren't knocking them dead before, what do you have to lose by trying something new?

Sal: Not much, I guess. But I'm uncomfortable not knowing

how everything fits together and whether I'll be able to handle it.

VP: If you're uncomfortable about what's going to happen in the future you're not alone. Just remember that **THE PRIMARY PRICE OF SUCCESS IS DISCOMFORT.** 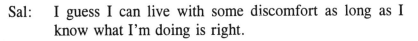 If you're not feeling uncomfortable when you're trying something new, you probably won't be successful at it.

Sal: I guess I can live with some discomfort as long as I know what I'm doing is right.

VP: There isn't any "right." In selling, the range of "right" is whatever works within a framework of **honesty** and **integrity**.

Sal: By the way, there's something I've been meaning to ask you. Can you give me some examples of some High Probability offers that people use in other businesses?

VP: Why?

Sal: Seeing some examples may help me to understand the process better and might make it easier for me to language my offer.

VP: Okay. I have two friends in other businesses who use the High Probability Selling approach. One sells insurance and the other works for a safety training company. I helped them language their offers. They say:

"This is John Boardman from the Protection insurance agency. I sell long-term care insurance, which covers the cost of nursing home care, or comparable at home care, not covered by Medicare. Is that something you want?"

"This is Jane Lewis from the Stay Safe safety training company. We conduct safety trainings which reduce accidents on and off the job by approximately sixty-five percent on an ongoing basis. Is this a service you want?"

Sal: I think I see. The offers are certainly clear and concise.

VP: That's just what you want.

Sal: Before we finish for now, I need to ask you about "commitments." Sue told me to ask you about the role "commitments" play in High Probability Selling.

VP: Good timing. Commitments are the foundation of High Probability Selling. If there is an art to our approach it's the way we structure our language to ask for commitments in a non-threatening way. Prospects are always given the option to say yes or no without any pressure. And we make it clear that we're satisfied with the prospect's decision, either way. We never attempt to manipulate a "Yes" answer.

The difficult thing for most salespeople to get is that we're just as satisfied with a "No" as with a "Yes." That's because we aren't **committed** to **"making the sale"** when we meet with a prospect. We're **committed** to the **High Probability Selling process**. We've been very successful with that approach. We have strong relationships with our customers and our salespeople feel good about what they're doing.

CHAPTER SIX

Target Marketing:
Identifying Niche Markets

Sal: Aren't all the companies that use product displays, prospective customers for WPC?

VP: Not really. They represent the potential market. But to be effective, you have to narrow the field and concentrate your effort. Since you only want to spend time with people who need, want and can afford our packaging, you have to do some preliminary work in order to save yourself time later on. But before you look for prospects you have to first see what your own company's strengths are.

Sal: What do our strengths have to do with identifying prospects? Don't our strengths have more to do with beating out the competition?

VP: No. The idea is to place yourself in a high percentage situation where you have the competitive edge. To do that, you have to match your strengths to those prospects who want your strengths the most.

Sal: How do you know what your market strengths are?

VP: No matter what the industry, there are three areas of market strength - Price, Quality and Service. Generally, in a competitive market, no company can provide all three concurrently.

Sal: What about something like on-time delivery? Which

area of market strength does that fall in?

VP: It depends. In the packaging business, on-time delivery is part of Service.

Sal: Isn't delivery time always part of the Service category?

VP: Think for a minute. If you were in the overnight delivery business, delivery would be your product. On-time delivery would be a measure of Quality. In that business, Service would include things like the accuracy of package tracking, billing, and courtesy.

Sal: What about a company that says it provides the best product, the best service and the lowest price? A lot of companies say that.

VP: Most of them are lying and they know it. As I said, it's virtually impossible to be the best in all three categories in a competitive environment. For example, high quality shoes are made with slow-tanned steer hide, and stitched with nylon. The manufacturer who uses plastic instead of leather will always be able to beat the price of a leather shoe manufacturer. The same holds true in any industry. It's almost impossible to excel in all three categories at the same time.

Sal: I see what you mean. There's a cost in providing excellent customer service, so a company providing high level service has to charge more than a company that doesn't.

VP: Right. The first thing you have to do is determine **your** company's strengths in the areas of price, quality and service. Then, when you're ready to sell, you'll have a better idea about which market segments best match up with your strengths. If you do that well, you'll save the time you might have spent with Low Probability Prospects.

Sal: But don't we always want to pitch WPC as having the best price, quality and service?

VP: No. The object is to sell the product you have and to sell it efficiently. The art is determining ahead of time what combination of quality, price and service you have, and then matching what you have with those segments of the market that need, want and can afford your particular combination of strengths. Our quality and service are excellent, but our prices are higher than many of our competitors.

Sal: Well suppose you have a customer who only wants to buy the lowest priced product and isn't interested in quality?

VP: Very unlikely situation. Give me an example.

Sal: What about a commodity like salt or sand?

VP: Well, let's say you have salt to sell, but it tastes bad or has a bad odor. You probably can't sell that stuff at any price.

Sal: I still might be able to if it's going to be used for melting ice or something like that.

VP: Not so fast. If your packaging leaks or tears, no one will ship it or store it, so you'll face an increased cost for packaging. And the people who handle it when it's being used have a vote too. Plus, using a lot of it in one area becomes a problem.

Sal: Okay, bad example. What about sand?

VP: Where are you marketing your sand?

Sal: Let's say you're selling to masonry contractors or road builders.

VP: Then purity and uniformity become important. If the sand has organic contaminants, masonry contractors won't buy it because the mortar will weaken when the organics decay. The same holds true for road building. It probably makes a big difference whether sand is wet or dry or whether it contains salts that affect the strength of the concrete. Even uniformity of color is probably important to some contractors.

Sal: How does service come into play when you're selling sand?

VP: If you're a masonry contractor service could matter a lot. Do you want to pick up the sand at the quarry or do you want it delivered to your job site? Do you want it in bulk or in bags? Do you want the sand delivered when you need to use it, or when it's convenient for your supplier to get it there?

Sal: I can see why contractors would be concerned about service under those circumstances. But do you think contractors really take quality and service into account when they're pricing out the cost of sand?

VP: Of course, they do. That's why it's important to "language your offer" in a way that addresses the needs and wants of your **target market**. For example, some masonry contractors want their sand delivered directly to the job site, in closely measured quantities and want it within hours of when it's going to be used. When the requirements of a group of prospects are that well defined, we call this segment a "market niche."

Sal: So, if the quality of your sand is okay, and you can deliver on time, you ought to be able to capture a good share of the sand market in your area.

VP: Yes, but that's only true if there's a sand market in your area that values those particular services. There may be a lot of contractors in your area who don't need or want those services.

Sal: Who wouldn't?

VP: What about a contractor who has his own dump trucks and would rather pick up than pay for delivery? Other contractors may have plenty of storage room at their job sites and not care if it's delivered early.

Sal: Identifying market strengths and niches sounds pretty complicated.

VP: Not really. It only seems complicated because neither of us knows much about contractors or sand. If we were working with contractors regularly, we'd either learn what their needs are or be out of business.

Sal: So now you're saying if we talked to a lot of contractors about their needs and wants, it would be easy to learn how to satisfy them and get their business.

VP: Maybe, but only if we were able to satisfy those needs and wants. If you know your own market strengths and find your niche, then it's easy.

Sal: Let me get back to packaging materials. We have to find out which prospects need our product. Right?

VP: Right, if you add the words "want" and "afford." Our customers have to want what we sell, and have to be able to afford it too. And, they have to want to buy it now.

Sal: That makes sense. Then my job is to find prospects who are ready to buy now.

VP: Right.

Sal: But if a prospect meets all of our other requirements, why don't you try to build a relationship with him now, even if he's not ready to buy yet?

VP: Because most good business relationships aren't built by hanging around or making small-talk over lunch. Business people who aren't looking to buy are usually too busy to spend time with salespeople. Besides, if you're too available or gratuitous with your time, people will think you're someone who doesn't value his time or capabilities. **Good business relationships are built on mutual respect, trust and two-way performance.** A customer isn't likely to change suppliers if the person he's already dealing with tells the truth and pretty consistently does what he says he's going to do.

Sal: Haven't all the other WPC salespeople already exhausted the available market niches?

VP: No. There are many undiscovered niches. First, look at the larger niche markets where WPC has a competitive advantage. Within that niche, every salesperson has to carve out a niche where he or she has some special skill or knowledge.

Sal: WPC's product niche seems to be consumer product companies who manufacture fragile products that need to be packaged and displayed.

VP: That's one niche where we have a definite competitive edge. But we're not limited to consumer products. We provide packaging for electronic components, appliance parts and lots of other products.

Sal: How did WPC get involved in so many areas?

VP: Over the years individual salespeople discovered niches that weren't being served. Some were obvious and others required knowledge of certain industries and creativity.

Sal: My problem is I've worked in the packaging industry for years. I really don't know very much about any other businesses.

VP: You know a lot more than you think! You worked in the graphic arts department of a packaging firm for a while, didn't you? You must know how art supplies are packaged.

Sal: Sure. I've worked with inks and specialty paper and small machinery and machinery parts too.

VP: How about your other packaging customers?

Sal: I understand. So all of my experience in packaging can be useful.

VP: Sure. Be a little creative with what you already know. It's time for you to get started with some prospecting on your own even though there are still some areas to go over. I'll talk with you in a couple of days.

SEVERAL DAYS LATER.

VP: How's it going?

Sal: Pretty good! I've been prospecting for the last few days and I've been getting better results since I trimmed my offer from fifty-nine words to forty-two. There's something I have to discuss with you. Sometimes when I'm prospecting, I can't resist the urge to sell.

VP: I'm glad you see that as a problem. It's a trap that most people fall into, especially experienced salespeople. The only way to stop selling (or persuading) when you're prospecting is to be aware you're doing it. Then stop doing it and get back to prospecting again.

Sal: How do you recognize you've started to sell?

VP: There are two basic tipoffs.

First, if you're prospecting and you start to feel stress, you've probably slipped into selling.

Second, if you find yourself on the phone with a prospect for more than three or four minutes, you're probably selling.

Sal: That's it?

VP: It's not as easy as it sounds. It takes a long time to train yourself to prospect correctly. Remember, it's not a tragedy if you slip occasionally, especially when you're first learning.

Sal: How long did it take you to eliminate selling from your prospecting?

VP: The truth is I still have a tendency to slip occasionally and I've been prospecting for years. But, when I find myself selling, I just go back to doing it right.

Sal: I feel better knowing it still happens to you.

VP: Just remember, if you language your offer properly, the prospect's responses will usually stop you from trying to sell.

Sal: I've had some trouble with some of the responses I've been getting. One prospect asked me why he would want to buy from me if he's happy with his current supplier.

VP: Whenever you get a response you don't know how to handle, there are at least two ways to reply: "I don't have a satisfactory answer to your question. What answer would make sense to you?" Or, "You don't sound like a High Probability Prospect. Is my product something you want, or not?" Both statements must be made in a flat, unemotional tone.

Sal: And that'll get me back in control of the prospecting process?

VP: Right. That also helps the prospect give you a "No" answer without any pressure or tension. If that happens you know you're dealing with a Low Probability Prospect.

Sal: But what if someone is really interested in our product?

VP: Look, there is no sales value whatsoever when a prospect says he's "interested." **There's no commitment in interest.** It's usually a cover for someone who doesn't want to buy. What matters is whether the prospect **wants** what you've got. When someone is really a High Probability Prospect you know it. You might miss one every once in a while. But we'd rather lose an occasional High Probability Prospect than waste a lot of time with Low Probability Prospects.

Sal: What do you say when you language your offer and a prospect says, "That sounds interesting."

VP: I would say something like, "Does that mean that you **want** what I'm offering, **or not**?" That's the question you have to get answered. You handle it the same way if a prospect responds to your offer by saying, "Maybe," or "I don't know," or "I don't think so," or "I'll consider it."

Sal: What if the prospect says, "Send me some information." What do you say then?

VP: My usual response is, "Usually when people say that, it's a polite way of saying 'Get lost'. If you want me to 'Get lost', just say so. It's okay." I don't send out information unless the prospect wants what I'm selling, needs the information and there's a strong likelihood that we'll do business after the prospect gets the information and reviews it.

Sal: What do you do when you're prospecting and the prospect starts getting defensive?

VP: When you're direct with prospects and not trying to manipulate them, they usually don't get defensive. In fact, High Probability Prospects usually identify themselves right away. Don't do any selling, persuading or anything else that can cause resistance. Just keep offering choices that allow prospects to disqualify themselves.

Sal: What do you mean?

VP: Just keep asking non-rhetorical questions. Ask questions that give the prospect the choice to say "yes" or "no."

Sal: And if you don't get a "no," then you pin down the appointment, right?

VP: Wrong! You let the prospect pin down the appointment. Say something like, "Do you want to get together to see if my packaging is what you want?"

Sal: Suppose he says he doesn't have time to get together.

VP: That's one way he dis-qualifies himself. If he doesn't have time, you don't either. He's a Low Probability Prospect.

Sal: Why? Maybe he just didn't understand what our packaging could do for him.

VP: If he doesn't know at that point and doesn't want to find out, he's a Low Probability Prospect.

Sal: Suppose he's just not aware of what we're offering?

VP: Then he's still a Low Probability Prospect. Either he's out of touch with his industry or isn't open to new ideas. That's a Low Probability Prospect.

Sal: How about if I ask someone whether he wants to meet to see whether our packaging is something he wants, and he says he won't be ready to meet for three months?

VP: Then ask him if he wants you to call back in three months.

Sal: So, I'm supposed to constantly throw the ball back to the prospect, right?

VP: That's the point! If the prospect makes all the decisions himself, without any persuasion or pressure from you, he feels responsible for those decisions and he won't say later that you talked him into anything.

Sal: This is completely different from anything I've ever done.

VP: That's true about all of High Probability Prospecting. Remember, consistently throw the ball to the prospect and let him be responsible for the outcome. While you're learning, you're sure to get a little confused. The best of us make mistakes, but with practice the process gets easier and easier.

CHAPTER SEVEN

Establishing a Relationship

Sal: I'm having a hard time with the High Probability concept you call "Establishing a Relationship."

VP: What's the problem?

Sal: I don't think I understand it. As soon as our salespeople meet new prospects, they start asking questions I'd never dream of asking. I think my biggest problem is that some of the questions they ask seem too personal.

VP: Do they get answers?

Sal: That's the point. I can't believe the responses. The prospects almost always answer the questions, even the most personal ones.

VP: Did any of them seem upset by the questions?

Sal: Only one.

VP: What happened?

Sal: I was on a call with Sue. When she started asking questions, the prospect gave her a look you wouldn't believe and then jumped all over her. Then Sue just got up and politely ended the call.

VP: Do you have a problem with that?

Sal: Sure. She got the guy upset and she didn't sell him anything.

VP: A call without a sale is no big deal. And even if the prospect hadn't gotten upset, there's a good chance Sue wouldn't have sold him anyway, so at least she didn't waste time trying.

Sal: How can you be sure if she had treated him differently she wouldn't have been successful? Besides, she already had the appointment.

VP: Being sure is not what this is all about. In High Probability Selling you don't wait to be sure. What matters is whether there's a high probability of making the sale or not.

Sal: That's what you said about prospecting. Besides, I thought Sue had already qualified the prospect before the call.

VP: The point is, even if you've qualified a prospect initially, you always give him an opportunity to disqualify himself. That's true at every phase. But let's get back to your question about "Establishing a Relationship" with a prospect.

Sal: Okay.

VP: For most salespeople Establishing a Relationship with someone is the most difficult and confrontive aspect of High Probability Selling. It requires the salesperson to forget about selling and just be a person. It's also the single most important step in High Probability Selling.

It's a time when you don't talk about your product at all. Your only purpose is to get to know the prospect and determine whether he's someone you can trust and respect. That decision is key because it determines whether you're willing to do business with him. You learn that through conversation and by asking questions.

When you don't trust and respect someone, it's very tough to hide it. If you don't, he'll know it almost as soon as you do, and **he** won't want to do business with **you**. But more importantly, you'll know it and **you** won't want to do business with **him**. If you try to do business with someone you don't trust and respect, you'll never have a workable relationship. And if the relationship isn't workable, it'll be difficult and unrewarding at best, forever.

In High Probability Selling we only do business with people we trust and respect. When you're Establishing a Relationship with a prospect, your purpose is to discover who the person inside the prospect is and how he got to be where he is, both personally and professionally. How you do that varies. Everyone's style is different.

In order to determine whether you trust and respect someone, you have to **really** get to know them - find out what makes them tick. What motivates them and why? What incidents or feelings shaped who they are? How they wound up in their current job? The search goes way beyond surface amenities.

It's not a matter of prying or trying to manipulate. You only have a limited period of time to spend on a call and you sincerely want to develop a relationship that means something. All meaningful relationships, professional or personal, are based on mutual trust and respect. If you can develop that kind of relationship with a customer you have such a competitive edge that is very difficult for anyone else to overcome. Everyone prefers to do business with someone they trust and respect. **If you don't develop that kind of relationship with a customer and get to know who he is, you're just another salesperson to him.**

In order to do what I'm suggesting, you have to be **sincerely interested** in the prospect. That kind of sincerity can't be faked. People know when you're asking questions and only pretending to be interested in the answers. When that happens the prospects will abruptly cut you short.

Remember, your purpose in discovering what makes a prospect tick isn't to uncover his "hot buttons" or what it will take to convince, persuade or manipulate him to buy. It's to see whether he's the kind of person **you're** willing to do business with - to see whether you trust and respect **him**.

To do that you probably have to operate in a way that's goes against everything you've been taught or conditioned to do in sales. You have to let go of "trying to please," "dancing to the prospect's tune," "getting him to like you," "being interested in what he's interested in" and "flattering him." You're not there to impress, entice, or "build rapport." You're not there to "get him to buy." You're there to **discover whether there's a mutually acceptable basis for doing business**.

Put yourself in his place. If you were the prospect and you felt that someone was **trying to get you to do something**, you would naturally try to protect yourself. That's where resistance, suspicion and hostility come from. Whatever the salesperson does or says in that kind of environment will be construed as manipulative, insincere and inevitably creates resistance.

Sal: Now I see why I always felt like I was in a war when I was selling.

VP: The problem lies with the fundamental definition of selling in our culture. "Selling" implies action to produce a result - convincing, persuading, enticing, and whatever else. Getting somebody to do something he might not otherwise do.

In High Probability Selling there's no selling, at least not the way selling is usually defined. You're there first and foremost to **discover whether there's a mutually acceptable basis for doing business.** When people sense you're not attached to a particular result, that you're not there to get them to do something, they start to trust you. When that happens you don't have to deal with suspicion, resistance and hostility.

But in order for someone to trust you, you must **be trustworthy.** It's not what you're doing, it's who you're being. Being truly interested in someone, communicates powerfully. **Who you're being speaks louder than your words.** When you're authentic, straightforward and not trying to get someone to do something, you're acting in a trustworthy fashion and the other person is likely to trust you.

Most people have difficulty weighing the merits of competitive offerings, which makes it doubly important for prospects to deal with someone they trust and can rely on. Salespeople invariably beat the drum for their products and tell prospects how wonderful their products are. Because every prospect knows that, they react by discounting just about everything the salesperson says. Yet at the same time, most prospects realize how little they really know in comparison to the vendors, and for that reason look to deal with someone they trust and respect.

Sal: All of this seems so unnatural.

VP: What we do in High Probability Selling is counter to what you would comfortably do. What's comfortable is what you've been conditioned to do. Traditional selling encourages fawning, flattery, feigned interest and insincerity. You're a product of that approach so you're comfortable doing it even though you don't feel very good about yourself when you do it.

Being interested in people, in what makes them tick, and how they got to be where they are, is very natural. That's how we were as children. Remember how you felt when you were little and someone moved in on your street. You probably wanted to know everything about them. You might've asked them, "Where did you live before? Why did you move here? Did you want to move? What does your dad do?" As we grew up we were taught to suppress our natural inquisitiveness in conversation, especially with people we've just met. But it's still there. It's just hidden, and most people aren't aware that it's there. The process of really getting to know someone is an enjoyable and rewarding experience. If you want to know what's natural, listen to the questions a four year old asks.

Sal: Every sales course I've taken emphasizes developing a rapport with the prospects. But I've never heard anything about really establishing a relationship with someone, especially one that has to do with trust. If I hadn't personally seen Sue and Sam do it, I wouldn't believe it could be done, especially in one meeting. The WPC salespeople I've watched were successful in establishing a relationship with most of the prospects they met. But I still can't believe the prospects **answered** the personal questions they were asked.

VP: The principle is simple. Almost everyone will answer just about any question you ask, truthfully and completely, if you genuinely want to know the answers and you're not being manipulative.

Sal: That's what Sue said. Why does it work that way?

VP: I honestly don't know, but I know from experience that it's true.

Sal: Maybe it's because...

VP: (interrupting) Don't waste your time trying to figure it out. A hammer is effective whether you understand why it works or you don't. Just use the tools the way they're designed if you want to be a master craftsman.

Sal: Okay. But for me it seems strange and pushy asking someone you've just met for that kind of information.

VP: Think about it this way. What you **want** to do in this situation is really get to know someone. Your purpose is to efficiently find out whether you can trust that person and respect him. If the answer is yes, you'll probably be able to develop a relationship that benefits both of you. Keep in mind too, the more you know about someone, the easier it'll be to provide him with what he wants.

Sal: That makes sense.

VP: On the other hand, if you find he's not trustworthy, you can move on before investing a lot of time.

Sal: But why are you so concerned about whether you trust a prospect? After all, we're only doing business with him.

VP: **You shouldn't do business with someone you don't trust or who doesn't trust you. It seldom pays in the long run.**

Sal: What could you learn about a prospect that would have you feel that way?

VP: You might learn the prospect has a history of giving vendors a run-around and giving very little in return, or that he has a relative or friend who sells for your competitor, and that he uses other people just to get information. Or you may learn he never pays vendors on time. Maybe he's just not being cooperative. Whatever the reason, if you sense you don't trust a prospect, leave right away, even if you can't articulate why you feel that way. Trust your gut on that.

Sal: Why would he tell you any of those things?

VP: When you're Establishing a Relationship with someone, they'll usually answer any authentic question you ask, and most of the time they'll tell you a lot about things you didn't ask.

Sal: Does Establishing a Relationship work to the prospect's advantage as well?

VP: What do you think the prospect is doing while this little exercise is going on? He's checking you out, too.

Sal: How does he do that?

VP: It just happens naturally. How we feel about another

person is usually a visceral reaction, sort of like intuition. If you're trustworthy it shows and the other person will know it. Not up here necessarily (pointing to his head), but down here (pointing to his stomach).

Sal: Since the prospect is usually doing most of the talking in High Probability Selling, it should be pretty easy for the salesperson to look trustworthy.

VP: Not really. It's pretty hard to fake who you are in High Probability Selling. If you're true to the approach, everyone involved has to be real or the call is a dud. That's one of the reasons you were tested before you were hired. We only hire people with the ability and inclination to be honest and straightforward.

Sal: But why don't prospects resist answering personal questions like the ones you ask? After all, they're complete strangers.

VP: Resistance comes from a sense of distrust. The process of Establishing a Relationship creates trust. Resistance never becomes an issue. When prospects speak openly and honestly with you about things that are personal to them, the further the conversation goes, the more trust they place in you. While that's going on, they're unconsciously very aware of your reactions. To maintain that atmosphere of trust you must be **sincerely interested** in what they're saying. Your purpose is to get to know them, **not to express judgements** about their ideas or feelings. **Just listen**. Being sincerely interested gets you there without any effort at all.

Sal: I can't believe that can all happen in one visit. It ought to take months or years to get close with someone.

VP: It happens or it doesn't on the first visit. That's when people are most receptive. That's the only time you start with a clean slate.

Sal: When I went out on calls I noticed that our salespeople didn't seem to have a set series of questions. Are there any questions you always ask?

VP: No, not in the Establishing a Relationship phase. When two strangers meet there's no way to predict which way the conversation will go. The idea is to generate a conversation that'll produce the information you need.

Sal: Making the transition from, "Hello, my name is Sal from WPC Packaging," to "Tell me about your wife and children," is awkward. It's just not natural to me.

VP: Come on, you know that's not how the conversation goes.

Sal: I guess it's mostly that I don't know what to say.

VP: It's really not what you ask that counts, it's whether you're interested in the answers. Look, I realize some of this seems difficult. If what I'm teaching you were obvious, or easy to figure out, we could save a lot of time and money on sales training. Some people do these things naturally. Most people have forgotten how to be natural or someone has taught them to be unnatural, and so what you're learning now has to be relearned and practiced.

I'll give you a few examples of the kinds of things I say to people when I first meet them. Try this approach with some of the prospects you've already identified.

When you first meet someone, make an observation about some aspect of his company, the building or about the location that **interests you.** Then attach a question to the observation. Something like:

> This is an interesting building. Did an architect design it?

> This looks like it might have been a textile mill a hundred years ago. How long has the company been here?

> It took me an hour to get here from my office. Are you from around here?

> Or ask something about how the prospect got to be where he is:

> How long have you been with the XYZ company? What did you do before that?

> How did you get started in this business? What did you do before that?

> How long have you been teaching Science? When did you first decide to become a teacher? Why?

As long as you keep asking questions that're based on the last answer, the prospect will most likely respond and get more involved in the conversation.

Sal: Give me an example.

VP: If a prospect says, "My first couple of years on the job were very difficult," ask him "Why?" .or "What was difficult about it?" or "What happened?" Don't reply to his statement with, "How many kids do you have?" or "Do you follow the Phillies?" Establishing a

Relationship is a **listening** skill. Listening to what the prospect says. When a person reveals something about himself that's personal, he's honoring you with his trust. If you don't respond with the kind of question that an "interested" person would naturally ask, you're indicating that **you** aren't really interested and that you're just going though the motions. At that point it'll be obvious to him that you're not worthy of trust.

Sal: Are there particular kinds of questions to ask?

VP: Yes. Ask open-ended questions like:

> Why?
> What did you do?
> How did you handle that?
> Was that something you wanted to do?

Open-ended questions give people an opportunity to express themselves, rather than answer Yes or No.

Sal: How do you know when you've completed the "relationship" phase?

VP: When you reach a point where you feel that you have a real sense of the person you're dealing with. You usually reach that point when the answers reflect sincerely personal, private kinds of responses. At that point you're inside. That's when you decide whether this is someone you want to do business with.

Establishing a Relationship with a prospect is important because that's when you determine whether you trust and respect him. Remember, you only do business with people you trust and respect. If the chemistry isn't there, end the visit politely but firmly.

Sal: How can you just walk out without taking a shot at selling him? You're there already.

VP: We've gone over this before, but I'll explain it one more time. Everyone's line has competition, so you usually have at least two salesmen trying to get the same business from a good prospect. Most of the time, products are pretty competitive. When that's the case, a prospect will buy from the person he trusts and respects. If you've been able to develop that kind of relationship, you'll get the business. If you don't have that kind of relationship, trying to sell that prospect is a waste of time.

Sal: Suppose a prospect interrupts while I'm Establishing a Relationship and wants to discuss my product?

VP: Tell him the truth. Explain that the way you do business is by learning about the prospect and his organization before discussing your product. Then ask him whether he's willing to continue in that direction or prefers that you leave.

Sal: How about if he just says, "Let's get down to business."

VP: Answer that by saying, "The way I do business is to learn as much as possible about my customers first. That way I know how to deal with them. I also need to find out whether I trust and respect them. I only do business with people I trust and respect. At the same time, my customers have a chance to make the same kind of determinations about me. So, are you willing to continue with this kind of conversation, or should I go?"

Sal: And if he's not, you leave?

VP: That's right. If he's not willing to answer your questions, disqualify him as a Low Probability Prospect.

Sal: But if you've done your prospecting right, this guy has already qualified as a High Probability Prospect?

VP: You always have the option of disqualifying a prospect. When a prospect is really willing to buy from you, he's almost always willing to talk and interact. High Probability Prospects generally want to have a relationship with you. It's very rare that a prospect who puts you off or is short with you later becomes a customer. Remember, first impressions are the ones that last. What the prospect puts out at your first meeting is what he wants you to get.

Sal: Don't people resent it when you tell them you only do business with people you trust and respect?

VP: Absolutely not. It's actually a **plus**. People don't respect, or want to do business with people who don't have standards. High Probability salespeople are very direct. Whenever a problem arises, they state their position and give the prospect a choice. Prospects appreciate being treated that way.

Sal: What if you're being trustworthy, but you sense that the prospect doesn't trust you?

VP: You should be able to figure that out by yourself. What else do you want to know?

Sal: The other WPC salespeople say that Establishing a Relationship is where the salesperson gets his "power." What do they mean by that?

VP: Unless you develop a relationship of trust and respect, you're just one more Willie Loman, with about the same chance of getting the order as your competition. When you develop a relationship, you have a commanding advantage over the competition. That advantage is your power. It's hard to describe. You just have to experience it for yourself.

Sal: Tell me if I have it right. **Establishing a Relationship with a prospect is a lot like having a conversation with someone you've just met socially, like at a party, with the sincere intention of finding out all about the other person.**

VP: Right. And the other person will find you interesting, mainly because you're interested in him. It's the same way in a social setting. Being interested has the same effect whenever you meet someone for the first time.

But that's not all there is to the sale. Once you've Established a Relationship you have to evaluate the prospect's commitment to the buying process. You do that by testing his willingness to make a series of commitments. That's the Discovery/Dis-Qualification phase.

Sal: How do you shift from the Establishing a Relationship phase to Discovery/Dis-Qualification?

VP: The shift takes care of itself. All you do is ask the first Discovery/Dis-Qualification question. There's really no transition. It may seem awkward talking about it, but in practice it's not. After you've seen it happen a few times, it'll be more comfortable for you.

CHAPTER EIGHT

Discovery/Dis-Qualification

VP: After establishing a relationship with a prospect, your next step is the Discovery/Dis-Qualification process. It doesn't take finesse or expertise to move into Discovery/Dis-Qualification. Once a prospect realizes you're **truly interested**, and not just trying to ingratiate yourself, he'll answer almost any authentic question.

Discovery/Dis-Qualification is simply a series of questions to determine whether there **is a basis** for doing business. The more detailed the answers, the more valuable the information you'll learn. If the prospect isn't willing to tell you what you need to know, you dis-qualify him.

The questions are of a general nature and not aimed at your product in particular. For example:

> Why do you need **this product**?
>   not
> Why do you need **our product**?

> Why do you need display packaging?
>   not
> Why do you need WPC display packaging?

The questions should be absolutely clear, to avoid any chance for misinterpretation. You should have the questions with you, written out, in the exact wording you intend to use. Write down the prospect's answers precisely. What he says and how he says it may be important later. Here are the Discovery/Dis-Qualification Questions:

(AUTHOR'S NOTE - Whenever the words "this product" are used, substitute your product or service.)

1.   Determine Need.

"Why do you need this product?"

They may or may not have a need. Whether they do or not, the question opens communication. Let the prospect give you his reasons for needing your product.

2.   Determine Want (Desire).

"Do you want this product?"

They may want it and not need it, or vice-versa. Either way, this is information you need. If the prospect answers, "Yes" ask:

"Why?"

The reasons may surprise you. Prospects usually give precise and detailed answers to this question. If they don't want your product, there's nothing more to discuss. End the meeting.

3.   Determine Financial Status.

"This product is going to cost approximately X dollars. Are you prepared to spend that?"

4.   Determine Time Requirements.

"If you decided to go forward, when would you want this to start?"

"What if it doesn't start then?"

5.   Determine Decision-Makers.

The Decisions-maker(s) is the person or people the prospect **consults** before he makes a decision to buy. Examples include his accountant, his boss, his partner or his spouse. A decision-maker doesn't necessarily have to have any formal authority.

"When you're making a decision like this, who do you usually like to talk it over with?"

After the prospect identifies his decision-maker(s), if there are any, you should say:

"I need to talk with them before I prepare a proposal. Are you willing to arrange that?"

If the prospect doesn't agree to that request say:

"That's not the way I work. I'm not willing to prepare a proposal unless I talk with them to find out what their concerns and objectives are. I'm not willing to prepare a proposal and have it rejected over a point that could have been handled up front. What do you want to do?"

6. Determine Authority.

    "If you decided to go forward, who else would have to agree?"

    When you're selling, it's important to know each person with authority to approve or reject decisions. You have to talk with everyone in that chain before you prepare a proposal. Handle this the same way you handled the necessity to talk with the decision-maker.

7. Determine Commitments.

    "What would happen if you don't purchase this product?"

    The answer to this question often provides interesting information. I once dealt with a prospect who confided that if our product wasn't delivered and installed on time, an assembly line would have to be shut down and it could cost him his job.

8. Determine Brand Preference.

    "Suppose you had to decide right now, without talking to me or anyone else, which brand would you buy?"

9. Determine Supplier Preference.

    "Is there someone would rather do business with?"

    He might not have a preference. But then again, he might have a brother-in-law in the business.

It's important to discover that as early as possible.

10.   Determine Internal Procedures.

"What's your procedure for issuing a purchase order?"

Take careful notes on their internal procedures and read those back to the prospect before you move on to the next question. Many orders have been lost because of ignorance of a company's internal procedures.

11.   Determine Personal Motivation.

"What would it mean to you personally, if you didn't purchase this product?"

It might not mean a thing, or it might mean something you'd never suspect. You'll never know if you don't ask.

12.   Determine Personal Prejudices.

"Is there any reason why you wouldn't want to do business with me? (pause) Something we haven't covered yet? (pause) An emotional reason? (pause) Anything?"

If there **is** something in the way, it's important to get it out in the open early on. Otherwise, you may end up doing a lot of work, and never learning why you didn't get the business.

13.   Determine Hidden Obstacles.

"What could be lurking in the background that would prevent this from happening?"

Sal: Some of these questions seem to be repetitive.

VP: That's partially true, but they're designed to expose and explore issues that need to be addressed. Each question probes a little differently. A prospect who trusts and respects you won't be offended. He'll actually try to interpret each question in a way that brings out new information. The questions are neutral. It's the responses that have personality.

Sal: What's the fundamental purpose for the Discovery/Dis-Qualification questions?

VP: There are really several purposes. The first is to **discover** important information you need to do business. Second, the answers may **dis-qualify** the prospect very efficiently. Third, each time the prospect answers a question and doesn't dis-qualify himself, your relationship with him improves and the level of mutual commitment increases. Finally, you get the opportunity to handle problems that could be deal-breakers if they happened to come up later.

Sal: Like what?

VP: Suppose you asked your prospect the question, "If you decided to purchase display packaging, who else would have to agree?" and he answered, "My partner would have to agree." What would you do then?

Sal: I guess I'd ask if it was okay to talk to his partner.

VP: Close, but not strong enough. The better approach would be to tell him that unless he arranges for you to meet his partner, before you get started, he'll be dis-qualified.

Sal: How would you say that?

VP: "I'll need to meet with your partner before I prepare a proposal. Are you willing to arrange that?"

Sal: What if he doesn't want to and says he'll present the proposal to his partner after it's completed?

VP: Your answer is, "That's not the way I work. You can't answer your partner's questions, I can. And I need to find out what his concerns and objectives are before I prepare a proposal. What do you want to do?"

Sal: Do you dis-qualify him just because he won't agree to let you meet his partner?

VP: That's right.

Sal: That's a tough position.

VP: It's not tough. It's smart and it's efficient. Tough doesn't get results. Having standards and being straightforward does.

Sal: What do you do when you don't understand a prospect's answer to one of your questions?

VP: Directly ask for a clarification. Say something like, "I don't understand what you just said. What did you mean?"

Sal: What if the answer seems evasive?

VP: Make sure the prospect understands the question, and no matter what happens don't move on until you're **fully** satisfied with the answer. The one you let slip by will be the one that comes back later on to haunt you.

Sal: What do you say if he really **is** being evasive?

VP: "You seem evasive, is there a problem?"

Sal: What if he still avoids answering your question?

VP: Tell him you won't move on until the question is answered.

Sal: Isn't that insulting?

VP: Quite the contrary. The fact that you're committed to what you're doing strengthens the prospect's respect for you.

Sal: How many ways are there for a prospect to dis-qualify himself in the Discovery/Dis-Qualification phase?

VP: Fourteen, one for each question.

Sal: Your overall emphasis seems to be on dis-qualification. Isn't it dangerous to focus on the negatives?

VP: No. What's really dangerous is ignoring the negatives. In the Discovery/Dis-Qualification process, the things traditional sales training programs refer to as "objections" are neutralized. Besides, true High Probability Prospects rarely allow themselves to be dis-qualified.

Sal: You only mentioned thirteen questions, but you said there were fourteen ways for a prospect to dis-qualify himself. Am I missing something?

VP: I'm saving one for last. What questions do you have up to this point?

Sal: There's something I'm confused about. I remember you or Sue telling me something about how High Probability salespeople "control the sales process." That's manipulation, isn't it? Whether you call it control or something else, won't the prospect recognize what you're doing and react with resistance? Don't people usually resist and resent being controlled?

VP: I'm sorry if we created any confusion. High Probability's concept of control is an important concept for you to understand. I should've been clearer about "control" when we first got started. **Asking questions puts you in control.** As long as you frame what you say as a question, you maintain control. Being in control means **controlling the sales process, not controlling the prospect**. When you ask questions, you're creating the agenda. At the same time, you prevent resistance by accepting the answers and answering the prospect's questions. As long as you're not being persuasive or manipulative, you won't create resistance.

Make it clear by your attitude that you want to deliver exactly what the prospect wants. At the same time, you have to be perfectly willing to leave if you learn the prospect won't be satisfied with what you can deliver. Even if he is satisfied with what you're offering, if he's not trustworthy or he's not being cooperative and open, you also have to be willing to leave. If you present yourself that way, sales resistance won't be an issue.

Sal: Is it because you establish a question and answer format from the beginning that the prospect is inclined to go along with you?

VP: Partially. But more importantly, it's the fact that you're straightforward about what you're doing, that you **really** want to know the answers to your questions, that you're not attempting to convince the prospect of anything and that **you're not there to get him to buy.** In other words, you're trustworthy and the prospect knows it. The prospect will consider you trustworthy if you conduct yourself in a way that is worthy of his trust. If that happens, the prospect is likely to go along with your format and trust the process.

Sal: Sounds like hard work.

VP: It takes practice to continually use a question and answer format, even when the questions are simple and direct. But doing that takes the prospect through the entire sale step by step, with his approval stated out loud, for both of you to hear, every inch of the way. Never move on to the next point until you get agreement on the current one.

Sal: Give me some examples.

VP: Suppose the prospect asks, "Can you print in metallic ink on exterior corrugated packaging material?" How would you respond?

Sal: Well, my old approach would have been to tell him that what he wants can't be done with present technology, and why it can't. Then I would've explained that WPC's top quality four-color process printing is more attractive than metallic printing. But that response doesn't ask a question. What's the better way to handle that?

VP: First, answer his question truthfully and directly. Then, rather than try to manipulate him, offer a choice and ask for a commitment.

Sal: I don't get it?

VP: Okay. Try this. "No, we don't print in metallic ink on the outside corrugated packaging. Metallic inks aren't durable enough to withstand handling. Will you accept a top quality four-color process, or must you have metallic printing?"

Sal: Well, that's practically inviting, "No, I must have the metallic." But if I could tell him about all of the other benefits of our packaging, he might change his mind and give up on the metallic.

VP: You're right. He might change his mind. But in High Probability Selling we're not willing to continue the sales process on the chance that we "just might" change a prospect's mind. If there's a high probability that the prospect won't buy from us based on a factor we can't change, we end the meeting and save the effort.

Sal: Well, your approach sure is consistent. So, by asking him, "Will you accept a top quality four-color process, or must you have metallic printing?" you either get agreement and commitment, or you end the meeting.

VP: Right. That's the essence of High Probability Selling. Require agreement and commitment every step of the way. If you maintain control by asking questions and require agreement and commitment at each step, you eliminate resistance and efficiently reach a conclusion that is satisfying to both parties.

Sal: Where was the commitment in the metallic ink example?

VP: The prospect could either accept what we sell or not buy from us.

Sal: And either answer is acceptable. I can see it'll take some discipline on my part to **accept** a prospect's decision not to buy. The salesman in me wants to try to make every sale.

VP: It'll take time and practice to change your thinking. But after you've tried this for a while, you'll see there's power in inviting prospects to say "No" when they mean "No."

Sal: What about question number fourteen, the one you left out?

VP: If every one of the first thirteen Discovery/Dis-Qualification questions have been answered to your satisfaction, and the prospect hasn't been dis-qualified, the fourteenth question is:

 "If I can meet all your criteria (or Conditions of Satisfaction) for this product, what will you do?"

Sal: Suppose he answers, "What do you mean?"

VP: Then you say, "What do you think I mean?"

Sal: That sounds a little arrogant.

VP: To whom?

Sal: Well, it sounds arrogant to me and I think most prospects would think it was arrogant, too.

VP: It sounds arrogant to salespeople whose approach has

always been to beg for an order. But it doesn't sound arrogant to High Probability Prospects. They know just what you mean.

Sal: What if the prospect answers question fourteen with, "I'll seriously consider doing business with you."

VP: You tell him: "That's not the way I work. I'm not willing to prepare a proposal unless I have a commitment that we'll do business if I meet your criteria. What do you want to do?" Unless the prospect clearly states that you'll get his business if you meet his criteria, you dis-qualify him.

Sal: Do I know enough yet to use this approach with the prospects I'm seeing next week?

VP: Not quite. We still have to review the principles of High Probability Closing.

CHAPTER NINE

High Probability Closing

Sal: I've been out on calls with our salespeople over the past few weeks, and tried to concentrate during the last few on High Probability Closing.

VP: Okay. Tell me what you think you've learned?

Sal: Well, by the time you get to High Probability Closing, most of the grunt work is already handled.

VP: After you've been using High Probability Selling for another few weeks you won't find any part of the process difficult or tedious.

Sal: Most of High Probability Closing seems a lot like traditional sales.

VP: Why do you say that?

Sal: From what I've seen, it looks like the salesperson is manipulating the prospect and the prospect looks like they're ready to do almost anything the salesperson suggests.

VP: It only looks that way. **Prospects are very cooperative at that point because of the relationship that's been created.** But the relationship can be destroyed in a second if you become manipulative. Manipulation is the enemy of trust and our approach requires trust on both sides.

In High Probability Closing, agreements and commitments are **negotiated** to establish a prospect's **Conditions of Satisfaction**.

Sal: Let me see whether I have everything straight. You don't start the Closing phase until a relationship is established, **and** until you've gotten satisfactory answers to all of the Discovery/Dis-Qualification questions. But you also said closing starts at the beginning of the sale.

VP: Closing does start at the beginning. First you establish the agenda by asking questions and offering choices. Each time the prospect chooses to go forward he's closing himself. On the other hand, when you reach what we call the Closing phase, you **precisely** establish the prospect's CONDITIONS OF SATISFACTION.

Once you get a commitment from a prospect on his Conditions of Satisfaction, the order is almost a certainty. Most people honor their commitments. Of course, you still have the job of meeting your customer's Conditions of Satisfaction.

Sal: What happens if a prospect doesn't honor his commitment?

VP: Then you're back to disqualification. In most businesses, there are enough prospects to let you refuse to do business with anyone who doesn't keep his word. In some industries, where there are only a limited number of prospects, you may have to continue to do what you can to deal with those kinds of people. That usually happens when your management thinks it's essential to do business with a particular company. But on a long term basis, dealing with people who don't honor their commitments is a losing proposition.

Sal: I've watched our salespeople establish Conditions of Satisfaction several times and they make it look pretty simple. They seem to have had a good idea of what the prospect wanted before they even started the process. A lot of the Conditions had already been handled during Discovery/Dis-Qualification.

VP: That's often true, but it's important to review the information covered in the Discovery/Dis-Qualification process and formally incorporate that information into the Conditions of Satisfaction. Have you noticed how the prospects generally react during the Close?

Sal: Establishing the Conditions of Satisfaction always seems to come down to a straightforward negotiation. The prospects were consistently cooperative. They never seem to give the salesperson the hard time I always had when I closed with traditional techniques.

VP: Why do you think that is?

Sal: Well, by the time the salesperson gets to the Closing phase, the prospects have already decided they want to do business. So they try to find areas of agreement instead of ways to say no. Because you're not pushing them to do something they don't want to do, there's no resistance.

VP: Very good. A relationship based on trust and respect lubricates the Closing process.

Sal: I can see that. Without the relationship you develop, closing would be the same nightmare it is in traditional selling. But in High Probability Closing there's no tug of war, so the interaction is actually relaxed and pleasant.

VP: Okay, how would you start the Closing phase?

Sal: First, I'd tell the prospect exactly what I'm doing. I'd say, "It's time to discuss your Conditions of Satisfaction. We'll write down exactly what you want, all your requirements. That's how I determine whether we can provide what you want. Are you willing to do that?"

VP: Well said. You offer the prospect a choice every time, a choice that allows him to say "No" if he chooses. Then what?

Sal: Then, I read back what he said about his needs and wants during the Discovery/Dis-Qualification process and ask whether that's correct and whether there's anything else he wants to add.

VP: Fine so far. What's next?

Sal: Then I get very specific about exactly what he will or will not accept.

VP: What do you say if he wants something we can't provide?

Sal: I tell him what we can do and what we can't. If we can provide him with an alternative, I offer that. **But I never try to talk him into anything and I never avoid telling him the negatives.**

VP: Okay. Then what?

Sal: Then I ask the prospect how we'll determine whether his Conditions of Satisfaction have been met. For instance, if he says he wants our packages to be "easy to set up," I ask, "How will you measure that?" or "Can we measure how easy they are to set up by seeing how long it takes one of your shipping clerks to set one up?" And I insist on an exact time measurement, say fifty seconds including taping. If a customer says he wants "vivid four-color art work," I ask him to sign a sample of the minimum quality he'll accept.

VP: Suppose he says he wants references from customers who use our packaging?

Sal: I ask how many references he wants and whether he'll call them in my presence. If he agrees, I ask what he'll do if he gets positive endorsements.

VP: Suppose you get that far and he says, "If that happens I'll give you an order." What then?

Sal: I've seen our salespeople do different things at that point. I'm not sure which one is correct.

VP: They're probably all correct, depending on the circumstances. By now you know High Probability Selling is a very precise process. So if they did different things at that point, they were probably handling different situations. For example, if price hadn't been discussed yet, you'd need to determine the acceptable price range. Something like, "When we discussed pricing, you said you wanted the advantages of point of sale advertising on your exterior packaging with no increase in cost. If we reduce your labor and storage costs, and lower your net overall cost for packaging, but your material costs are higher, what will you do?" If his answer is, "I'll buy provided there's a net savings," you can go on to the next step.

Sal: What's the next step?

VP: Do the numbers. Determine precisely how much he'll save in labor and storage costs and how much is left for materials. He needs to see that number and commit to an order if our price for material produces a net savings. But remember, **never ask for the order**.

Sal: As many times as you've told me that, it still doesn't sound right. Asking for the order was what sales was always all about. But the WPC salespeople usually say something like, "If our price comes in below that figure, what will you do?" or "If we can set up in less than fifty seconds, what will you do?"

    Why not just come right out and ask for the order? When they say it your way the prospect seems to struggle for an answer. It's about the only time that any part of the process gets awkward.

VP: Who is it awkward for?

Sal: For the prospect, and for me when I'm watching him.

VP: It seems awkward because the prospect is reduced to two choices, commit or end the process. The approach puts the prospect in a position where **he has to generate the commitment**, not just accept the salesperson's request. Generating the commitment is something he probably hasn't had to do before. He's in uncharted waters without a compass. So he finds it a little awkward adapting to the freedom you've given him.

Sal: That's an interesting way to look at it - "Freedom."

VP: But that's exactly what it is. In traditional selling when the salesperson "closes," the salesperson feels like he's won and the prospect feels like he's lost. The prospect may feel relieved the sale is over, but he isn't comfortable. In High Probability Selling the prospect feels like he's won too. Because he wasn't pressured, and generated his own commitment, the prospect knows the decision was his. When it happens that way, you rarely see "buyer's remorse" and canceled orders.

Sal: What I used to do at that point is thank him for the order and leave. I was taught that more conversation at that point can "un-sell" the prospect. But WPC salespeople keep drilling the prospect even after he's committed.

VP: What do you mean "drilling" him?

Sal: You know. When he says, "I'm ready to give you an order," they say, "Are you sure that's what you want to do?" or they ask, "Why?" It sounds like they try to talk him out of the sale.

VP: You're missing the point. What we do is designed to test his commitment and allow him to strengthen it.

Sal: Why bother? Can't further conversation change a prospect's mind?

VP: It could. But if he's going to change his mind, when do you want to find out about it? When you get back to the office and find a message from him? Wouldn't you rather find out while you're still with him, so you can deal with his concerns?

If his commitment is weak, the best thing to do is find out why, right then and there. Wouldn't you rather handle problems in person than have to deal with them later by phone?

If his commitment is strong, a discussion won't shake it.

In fact, when you ask the prospect, "Are you sure?" or "Why?" he'll probably give you his real reasons for making the commitment, reasons he hasn't even talked about yet. In the process, he reaffirms and strengthens his commitment.

Sal: Let me shift gears for a minute to ask a question. Yesterday, I went out with Stan to a large toy manufacturer. After reviewing the buyer's Conditions of Satisfaction, Stan said, "I'm sure we can meet all your Conditions of Satisfaction. When would you like me to come back and demonstrate that to you?" The prospect set a date for the following Tuesday. Then Stan said, "When we demonstrate that we can fulfill all your Conditions of Satisfaction on Tuesday, what will you do?"

The answer was, "I'll give your proposal serious consideration."

Stan said, "That's not the way I work. I won't prepare a proposal unless I have your commitment to do business if I meet your Conditions of Satisfaction. If you're not serious about buying if we fulfill your Conditions of Satisfaction, just say so. It's all right to say 'No,' if that's what you mean. Just say so now, not after I've done all the work."

Then the buyer said, "Do you expect a commitment before I've seen your proposal?"

Stan answered, "I think it's fair for you to make a commitment to do business if I demonstrate I can meet all of your Conditions of Satisfaction. If that's not what you want to do, it's okay."

Then this guy said, "Other salespeople knock themselves

out and don't ask me to do anything, let alone commit at this point. They're happy to have the opportunity to show me their stuff. Why should I give you a commitment?"

Stan looked this guy right in the eye and said, "You don't have to make a commitment unless you want to. But I won't prepare a proposal for you without one. So, what do you want to do?"

The prospect looked stunned, like he couldn't believe what Stan was saying. "Okay," he said, "I'll give you an order if you show me you can meet all my Conditions of Satisfaction."

Why did Stan give the guy such a hard time? What was he doing? It looked very risky to me.

VP: Before I answer you, I'd like to hear how Stan's discussion ended. I'm sure it didn't end where you stopped.

Sal: When the buyer said, "Okay, I'll give you an order if you show me you can meet all my Conditions of Satisfaction," Stan said, "Are you sure that's what you want to do?" And the guy said, "Yes, I'm sure."

VP: And...?

Sal: Then Stan said, "Why?" I couldn't believe it! Stan had the guy closed, then he opened things up again.

VP: Did "Why?" get an answer?

Sal: It sure did. The prospect went on to give a bunch of reasons why he wanted WPC to be his packaging supplier, and why he liked the way Stan did business.

Then Stan said to him, "Is there any doubt in your mind, that if I come in next Tuesday, and demonstrate we can meet your Conditions of Satisfaction, that you'll give us your order?"

And the buyer smiled and said, "No, Stan, there's no doubt and it'll be my pleasure."

VP: So, about your question, "Why did Stan give the guy such a hard time?" can you answer the question yourself?

Sal: Well, Stan said he wanted to be sure the commitment was real, that it was clearly the prospect's choice and not because he was manipulated or persuaded. He wanted the prospect to say it was what **he** wanted, not what Stan wanted.

VP: Did that happen?

Sal: It did.

VP: What do you think the chances are of a prospect backing out of that kind of commitment?

Sal: Not much. That's the exact opposite of what they call "Assuming the Close;" the approach so many of the sales courses teach.

VP: High Probability Selling requires mutual respect between the salesperson and the prospect. The manipulation inherent in the "Assumptive Close" is totally out of place when you respect the prospect and he trusts you.

From beginning to end we offer the prospect a choice which includes his right to choose "No." If he chooses "Yes," then he's making a commitment and we proceed.

If he chooses "No," we dis-qualify him and conserve our resources for prospects willing to make commitments.

Sal: The fact that we don't show the prospect our product, or even tell him about it, or make up a quote or proposal **until after he has made a commitment to buy**, is different too.

VP: Very different.

Sal: So, we eliminate all the demonstrating and convincing that's usually done before the close.

VP: You've got it.

Sal: I still have the urge to convince prospects to change their minds when they won't commit.

VP: You'll get over that in time.

Sal: I've actually been trying to convince prospects to do something they don't want to do for most of my career. No wonder they've been resistant.

VP: That's why traditional selling is so hard and ineffective. If it were effective, you'd still be at your old job.

Sal: I guess it's hard to break old habits. But I think I'm getting there.

VP: I agree, but I can tell by your comments that sometimes you forget High Probability Selling is a dis-qualification process. Don't try to close every prospect you contact. The approach is to dis-qualify the Low Probability Prospects, which most are, quickly and efficiently, and spend most of your time and resources on High

Probability Prospects. Most of them, you'll close.

Sal: I guess it's about time I started earning my pay by going
        out and getting my own accounts.

VP: Go to it.

CHAPTER TEN

Some Fine Points

Sal: I went on three appointments yesterday and every prospect wound up dis-qualified. When I made the appointments each one sounded like a High Probability Prospect. But none of them was willing to make the commitments necessary to go forward with the sale. I can't figure out where I went wrong.

VP: What makes you think you went wrong?

Sal: I've got to be doing something wrong. When the other WPC salespeople meet with High Probability Prospects, they usually nail down a sale on the first visit. I was zero for three.

VP: Well, let's take a look at the possibilities. First, you were on your own for the first time. You're new with our company, and calling on new customers with a technology that's brand new to you. I consider it a plus that you came back in one piece.

Second, your prospects may have only seemed to be High Probability Prospects. When you have more experience in High Probability Prospecting, you'll be much better at recognizing and dis-qualifying Low Probability Prospects on the phone. But, take it from me, no matter how long you've been at it, no one bats a thousand.

Third, you probably made some mistakes. Sometimes

you get lucky in the beginning, but if you do, that's not always to your advantage. Good luck early on sometimes interferes with real progress. You learn more from the mistakes.

Sal: What do you mean?

VP: Once in a while, prospects buy even when you do everything wrong. We call that **"Random Negative Reinforcement."** That kind of success sometimes reinforces approaches that are ineffective in the long run.

Sal: That might be a problem for someone who's new to selling, but I've been doing this for years. I know most of the traditional selling techniques and how infrequently they work. I don't think there's much danger of me being a victim of Random Negative Reinforcement.

VP: Just keep it in mind. Everybody's susceptible to it to some degree.

Sal: Okay. I have two appointments this morning and after that I plan to spend the rest of the day prospecting.

VP: Good. I know prospecting probably isn't much fun yet. But believe me, at some point it actually becomes enjoyable.

Sal: I just want to be productive. Right now, I feel frustrated.

VP: Just don't make the mistake of being so anxious that you schedule appointments with prospects who don't qualify.

THE NEXT DAY

Sal: I saw my two prospects yesterday. The first one I dis-qualified. The second one asked for a quote on packaging for a new product line. When I got back from the call I told Sue what I needed, but she said she wouldn't ask the estimating department to quote it. What's that all about?

VP: What did the prospect say he would do if you gave him the quote?

Sal: He said if our price was right he would put my quote into his budget. And then, when they get into production, he said he would give us their business.

VP: Talk to Sue about giving him a "budgetary quote." We can work up budgetary quotes without much effort or expense. They're really "guesstimates" based on estimates of production quantity, order size and other stuff that always changes by the time companies are ready to order.

Sal: But this guy wants a quote with precise pricing on every option.

VP: Let me guess. He wants a quote for every quantity from prototype to full scale production, doesn't he?

Sal: How did you know?

VP: You better evaluate the probability of getting his business before we do all that work.

Sal: But how can we get his business if we don't give him a quote?

VP: How do you know you'll ever get his business if you haven't gotten his commitment to do business with you?

Sal: How can I get him to make a commitment without first telling him the price?

VP: You can't get him to do anything he doesn't want to do. All you can do is offer him a choice. You could've asked him, "Assuming the price is acceptable, what will you do?" It looks like you didn't do a thorough job determining whether he was committed to doing business with us if we met his Conditions of Satisfaction.

Sal: He really didn't give me a chance. I got through the Discovery/Dis-Qualification questions without any problem. But then he started telling me all the things he wanted and right after that he asked me to get him a quote.

VP: And that's when you started to "dance."

Sal: What do you mean by "dance?"

VP: What does it sound like?

Sal: Like I did whatever he asked me to do. He led and I followed.

VP: Right. How did you get into that position?

Sal: I guess I lost control.

VP: Sounds that way to me.

Sal: Where did I go wrong?

VP: You stopped asking your questions and started answering his.

Sal: You're right, but I didn't know how to get back into a questioning mode?

VP: The question is how you got out of that mode in the first place. Did you ask for a commitment as soon as you completed the dis-qualification questions?

Sal: No. The Discovery/Dis-Qualification questions went so well, I felt sure he wanted to do business with me. So I went along with him instead of asking for his commitment at that point.

VP: What was your basis for expecting he would do business with you when he hadn't made a commitment to you?

Sal: I felt we had a good relationship, and he was acting like he wanted to do business with me.

VP: He may have felt that way at the time. But, until a prospect makes a definite commitment, you don't know whether he's committed or not. And he isn't likely to make a commitment unless he's offered the choice to do so, or not.

Sal: That sounds like the old "Always ask for the order" routine.

VP: You seem to have a real hang-up about that. By now you have to know that asking for a commitment is not "asking for the order."

Sal: I'm not really hung up about that. It's just hard keeping the concepts separated. The difference is very subtle.

VP: No, it's not. In High Probability Selling we give the prospect the choice of "Yes" or "No." In traditional selling you give the prospect the choice of "Yes" or "Yes."

Sal: I guess I blew it. Is it too late to go back and ask for a commitment?

VP: No. It's never too late to ask for a commitment. But it's a lot harder after you've lost control. Work up his budgetary proposal and ask for a commitment when you present the quote. If he makes a commitment, you'll still come out fine. If he doesn't, chalk one up to experience.

THE NEXT DAY

Sal: I saw three prospects yesterday. I dis-qualified the first one after about fifteen minutes.

VP: Why?

Sal: He actually dis-qualified himself. Instead of answering my questions, he kept interrupting saying he would only consider us as a supplier if we made up samples for him to see.

VP: And what did you say?

Sal: I said we might be willing to make up samples if we understood what he needed and wanted and if we had a commitment from him. Then, before I could tell him what kind of commitment we needed, he told me he doesn't make commitments until he's convinced he's getting the best design, the highest quality and the lowest price. So I said, "That's not the way I do business," and I left. I was really angry.

VP: You did the right thing by ending the meeting at that point. The only problem seems to be your reaction to what happened.

Sal: Why is that?

VP: Why should you get upset with someone because he's a Low Probability Prospect? That's like getting angry because he's short. That's just what he is. Just realize there **are** Low Probability Prospects, recognize them when you meet them and move on.

Sal: I guess you're right. At my last job, I would've been suckered into trying to please that guy by trying to do whatever he wanted. I used to spend a lot of time and effort "dancing" for Low Probability Prospects.

VP: How did your other two appointments go?

Sal: At the second one, I established an excellent relationship. Then, during the Discovery/Dis-Qualification questions the prospect told me she wouldn't actually be ready for new packaging for about six months. That didn't make sense because when I called to make the appointment, she said the company wanted a new packaging design right away.

VP: So, what did you do?

Sal: I asked her about the discrepancy. She told me they were starting to collect ideas for a new product line but they wouldn't be ready for production for another six months. At that point I asked her whether she wanted to do business with me or not. She said, "Definitely, provided your packaging is right for my product." Then she asked for samples and price quotes.

VP: Then what happened?

Sal: Well, I asked her if we could define her Conditions of
        Satisfaction and, on that basis, arrive at a mutual
        commitment.   She said she couldn't make any
        commitments until they were ready to make final
        decisions on their packaging. She said that wouldn't
        happen for about six months.

VP: What did you say to that?

Sal: I asked whether she wanted me to get back to her then.
        She said I should stop back in about five months to
        familiarize myself with their marketing plans, meet the
        other people involved in the project and see what they
        wanted.

VP: It sounds like you made the most of that call. There's
        nothing you can do when the timing's wrong. Sounds
        like you were misled a little on the phone but the call
        may still be productive. Make sure you mark your
        calendar and get back to her. What about your third
        prospect?

Sal: I saved the best for last.   After Establishing a
        Relationship and asking the Discovery/Dis-Qualification
        Questions, I asked the company's advertising manager,
        "If our packaging gives you attractive point of sale
        advertising, and doesn't cost much more than your
        current packaging materials, what will you do?"

        He asked, "How much more will your packaging cost?"

        I said, "About one dollar more per unit."

He said, "If that's all it'll cost, I'll buy your packaging. Will you make up some samples?"

So I said, "I can show you samples of similar packaging we've made for other customers, but we don't make up custom samples without a commitment. If you'll give me an order for a sample run, I'll credit the cost against your first production order. Are you willing to do that?

And he said, "Sold! Let's write up a purchase requisition, so you can get started right away."

We wrote up the requisition together. Then we went over to the purchasing department, got the order typed and I walked out with it in my hands. I loved it!

VP: Congratulations! How do you feel about High Probability Selling now?

Sal: It's great. I think I'm starting to get the hang of it.

VP: You are, but you still have a lot to learn. On that last call, you apparently didn't feel the need to take your prospect through his Conditions of Satisfaction after getting his commitment to give you his business. All your sales won't be that easy.

Sal: That didn't even occur to me.

VP: Once you've established a relationship of trust and respect with a prospect he'll usually **want** to do business with you. Still, most prospects want to be **certain** that their specific needs and wants will be met before giving you a purchase order.

Sal: He was so sure we would do the job right, he just gave me the order.

VP: Not exactly. You told me the two of you wrote up the purchase requisition. How did you go about that?

Sal: I see what you're driving at. While we were writing up the requisition I handled his Conditions of Satisfaction. We went over everything he wanted, what we would do, what we wouldn't do, and then we discussed what was acceptable to him. It went so smoothly I didn't realize what was going on.

VP: Did you feel like you were manipulating him?

Sal: Not at the time. While I was there, I felt like we were just "doing business." After I left, when I thought about how easy everything went, I did have a thought that I manipulated him. But now that I see how we worked out the details together when we wrote up the purchase order, I realize I didn't influence him to do anything he didn't want to do. In fact, he was very careful to point out exactly what he wanted.

VP: It's important to fully understand what you just said. It's also important for **you** to handle the prospect's Conditions of Satisfaction. It's your responsibility to do that, and to do it openly and thoroughly.

      Remember - **if you feel you're being manipulative, the prospect is feeling it also**.

Sal: What can you do if that happens?

VP: Just what I told you before. Recognize it, and then stop it. Then ask whether what you were discussing is what he wants.

Sal: You know, until last month I wouldn't have dared to do that. I would've been afraid to break the spell, and afraid he would say "No."

VP: What most salespeople forget is a prospect can always say "No." If you persuade him to say "Yes," when he really means "No," he'll probably cancel on you the next day.

Sal: I see I still have a lot to learn about High Probability Selling.

VP: Do you understand enough about Conditions of Satisfaction to go through them properly with your next High Probability Prospect?

Sal: I think so. But I don't feel very comfortable with that yet.

VP: You know what discomfort means, don't you?

Sal: Sure. Discomfort indicates progress and growth.

CHAPTER ELEVEN

Conditions Of Satisfaction and Some Review

Sal: Good morning.

VP: What's hot?

Sal: Well, over the past week I've tried to only make appointments with High Probability Prospects. I've had some really interesting calls and I sold another new customer. But I'm still having trouble dis-qualifying Low Probability Prospects.

VP: What's been going on?

Sal: I find Establishing a Relationship with the prospect more and more natural. Really getting to know new people every day is a real plus. But I find that once I Establish a Relationship with a new prospect, it's hard to abruptly end the appointment if it turns out he's a Low Probability Prospect.

VP: You don't have to end it abruptly. Just be polite and tell the prospect why you're leaving.

Sal: That's not the problem. It's that I've invested a lot of time and effort getting to know the prospect, and I **feel** like I should stay and see if it's still possible to work something out.

VP: It sounds like you're still trying to sell **every** customer.

Sal: Maybe I am but it's hard to change, especially when you like the prospect and want to do business with him.

VP: Try remembering why you're there - to determine whether there's a mutually acceptable basis for doing business. Your time is valuable.

Sal: I also find myself trying to be persuasive sometimes.

VP: When do you notice yourself being persuasive?

Sal: It usually comes up while I'm going over the customer's Conditions of Satisfaction. I want to close on every point, and sometimes I want to talk prospects out of any conditions we can't meet.

VP: High Probability Closing should be the easiest part of the sale. Remember, manipulation arouses resistance. Let's go over everything from the top.

First you Establish a Relationship. Once that's complete you'll know whether you want to do business with that person. If you're not sure whether you have mutual trust and respect, dis-qualify the prospect and leave.

If you're still there, ask the Discovery/Dis-Qualification Questions. Every question has to be answered and every problem has to be resolved to your satisfaction. All of the decision makers, including the person with the authority to say yea or nay, have to be included in the process.   Then tell the prospect you need to precisely establish his Conditions of Satisfaction. In other words, each of the criteria that must be met for him to buy.

Then you ask, "If I come back with a proposal that meets your Conditions of Satisfaction, what will you do?" If he says anything other than something like, "I'll give you my business," you set out your ground rules. Tell the prospect it'll take a good deal of effort to demonstrate that your offering will meet his Conditions of Satisfaction, and that you're willing to demonstrate that only if he makes a commitment to give you his business provided you meet his Conditions of Satisfaction. If he doesn't willingly make a clear and definite commitment, dis-qualify him.

After he makes a commitment, ask for each and every Condition of Satisfaction he requires and record each one in his exact words. Bring up any conditions he hasn't mentioned that need to be addressed. Negotiate any conditions you can't meet. If there are conditions you can't satisfy, and they can't be negotiated, dis-qualify him. If you arrive at a set of Conditions of Satisfaction you can meet, you have a deal. At the next meeting present a proposal that demonstrates you can meet his Conditions of Satisfaction, and complete the transaction.

Sal: You mentioned something just now that's been a problem. When one of the Conditions of Satisfaction is something we can't meet.

VP: Give me an example.

Sal: Well, one prospect told me he wanted to buy our packaging, but wouldn't pay more than ten percent over their current packaging costs. When I told him we couldn't do that, the deal died.

VP: Why is that a problem?

Sal: I didn't get a chance to show him the advertising value of our displays.

VP: Maybe he had valid reasons for deciding our packaging was only worth ten percent more. Did you ask him his reasons?

Sal: No. I just assumed he was being difficult, so I dis-qualified him and left.

VP: You may have been right. It's hard to know without having been there. I probably would've asked "Why?" It's better to ask "Why," than try to guess what someone is thinking. In any case, it's still good strategy to dis-qualify any prospect you have doubts about. **A High Probability Prospect will seldom allow himself to be dis-qualified without a struggle.**

Sal: Maybe I should've tried to entice him a little by asking something like, "Would you like to increase your sales by thirty percent like sixty percent of our customers have?"

VP: Don't do that. Those rhetorical questions are openly manipulative and insulting. In High Probability Selling, whenever you feel persuasive, convincing or manipulative, you know you're not following the basic principles. Give it some thought and you'll realize where you went off track.

Sal: But I want the customer to understand how much our packaging will improve his sales. If everyone in our target market knew that, I bet they'd all use WPC.

VP: You're kidding, right?

Sal: But over sixty percent of our customers do report at least a thirty percent sales increase with our aisle displays.

VP: That's true. But, the customers who use our displays get good results because they carefully analyze whether our products will do them any good. Not every customer would get the same results or be able to justify the increased cost.

Sal: I hadn't thought about that. If they don't have the right aisle location we may not be cost effective.

VP: Right.

Sal: But where our product does have a definite benefit, how do you point that out?

VP: It's not necessary. Most prospects generally know what the benefits of our packaging are. If they didn't, you wouldn't be there talking to them. They probably don't know the costs, our art and printing capabilities or other fine points. But our prospects are usually aware of what's available to increase sales. If they don't know what's going on then they're Low Probability Prospects.

Sal: Why do you make a written list of the prospect's Conditions of Satisfaction?

VP: When you list the Conditions of Satisfaction, you are, in effect, shaping the terms of an agreement. If you can deliver what they want, when they want it, at an agreed upon price, you'll get a commitment. **A primary goal is to eliminate ambiguities so there are no reasons for the prospect to renege later on.**

Sal: But if we offer to guarantee satisfaction, the buyer has nothing to lose.

VP: That's precisely what we never do. Some people can never be satisfied. Never guarantee unconditional satisfaction. We simply limit demands by listing the prospect's Conditions of Satisfaction.

Sal: What's the best condition to start with?

VP: There's isn't any "best" number one. You have to resolve the primary areas - price, service and quality. You can start with any of them. Most salespeople like to leave price until last, but that's not the way we work. You've already qualified the prospect on price during the Discovery/Dis-Qualification process, so price is usually as good a place to start as any.

Service is an area where you have to be very explicit. Handle what you will and won't do. That includes the prospect's delivery schedule, after-sale service, what extras he'll have to pay for, what happens if he has trouble with the product and anything else that applies to your offer.

Quality includes the features of your product. For WPC salespeople it includes the type and quality of the printing, the size, the color and strength of the packaging, the time and ease of assembly and any other physical characteristics.

Spell out the prospect's Conditions of Satisfaction in detail so that later, you can measure your performance.

Sal: So when you demonstrate your product, you can confirm it's what he's already committed to buy.

VP: Right.

Sal: Okay. If I were selling insurance instead of packaging, I would find out the prospect's financial needs while we were discussing his Conditions of Satisfaction, and then match a product to his conditions.

VP: Right.

Sal: Isn't that what they call "needs selling" in the insurance
        business?

VP: Not at all. Insurance agents usually try to get financial
        information before they tell the prospect what they're
        selling. Then they try to convince the prospect he has
        needs he wasn't even aware of. Then the agent tries to
        demonstrate how his product will satisfy those needs.
        The approach is a grind with a low probability of
        success.

        **We only deal with prospects who know they need the
        type of product we offer, and want to satisfy that
        need now**. So while we're establishing the prospect's
        Conditions of Satisfaction, we can be very specific about
        the product the prospect is agreeing to purchase. Most
        people in the insurance industry don't know how to find
        that kind of prospect, and when they do, they often have
        difficulty dealing with him effectively.

Sal: Give me some help on a problem I had with a customer
        named Joe Raffia at GHI Manufacturing.   After we
        negotiated his Conditions of Satisfaction, I came back to
        the office and had the estimating department work up a
        quote. Then I looked around and found some packaging
        samples we had prepared for one of our other
        customers. It's construction and art work were similar
        to what Joe said he wanted. I met with him the next
        day to go over the quote and demonstrate the samples.
        My quote was in line with his budget and he said he was
        satisfied with the quality of the printing. At that point
        I asked whether he wanted me to assist him in writing
        up the order with his purchasing department. He told

me it was too soon for that. He said his marketing manager had to approve the art work and that it would be a couple of months before that would happen because that's when they're starting their new advertising campaign.

VP: What's Joe's job title?

Sal: He's the Product Manager for their Non-Dairy Dessert line.

VP: Did you talk to the division marketing manager and the sales promotion manager?

Sal: No. When I asked Joe if he was the decision-maker, he said he had complete responsibility for all aspects of the line. But that wasn't the truth.

VP: Don't blame the prospect when something goes wrong with the sale.

Sal: Are you saying I did something wrong?

VP: **If you don't take responsibility for your results, you won't discover your errors and you'll keep repeating them**. I'm not saying if you do everything right you'll always get the sale. Selling isn't a science. High Probability Selling is effective, but not foolproof. And yes, in this case you did several things wrong.

Sal: What?

VP: You replaced two of the Discovery/Dis-Qualification questions with one of your own. And when you asked Joe if he was the decision-maker, he side-stepped your question and gave you an evasive answer - a non sequitur. You accepted his non-answer.

Sal: I wanted to find out whether I was dealing with the decision-maker. So I thought I should just ask him that question.

VP: There's a lesson here. In the future, if you don't understand something, ask. We're very precise about what we say to prospects. Each question has a purpose. If your way worked we would use it.

Sal: What's wrong with asking someone if he's the decision-maker? What if I asked the question and didn't allow him to get away with a non sequitur for an answer. What if he just answered, "Yes?"

VP: The question you asked invites a misleading response. It's vague and open to misinterpretation. The questions in the Discovery/Dis-Qualification process are:

    1.   When you're making a decision about whether to change your packaging, who do you like to talk it over with?

    2.   If you decide to go forward, who else would have to agree?

Sal: I can see the difference. There's really no room for misinterpretation with those questions.

VP: The order of the questions and the precise language are very important. The wording is designed to elicit the exact information you need. The problem you had with Joe had nothing to do with the Conditions of Satisfaction. It had to do with the questions you asked in the Discovery/Dis-Qualification phase.

Sal: I hate to keep telling you about my failures but that's the only way I'm going to learn. I had a problem with

Michael Benson at Benson Wall Covering. He's the grandson of the company's founder. He's vice-president of sales promotion and he's in charge of point-of-sale advertising.   At our second meeting I presented a proposal and showed him sample packaging for their wallpaper rolls. I made a mock-up by gluing a swatch of his wallpaper to a section of the display header, and then placing a copy of one of their magazine ads above it.

VP: Sounds inventive.

Sal: When I showed him the mock-up he said he didn't like the magazine ad. He was the one who gave it to me. I asked him why he didn't like it.   He said the advertising agency that had done the color separations for the ad didn't match the wallpaper colors in the ad with the actual color of the swatch. He said if the swatch and the ad were on the same box, the colors had to match exactly. I jumped on that! I asked him what he meant by "exactly." He said the match had to pass his personal inspection. I told him I could guarantee that our color match would meet industry standards. For any critical color, we would give him two samples to set the limits of the color range.

Then he said he had to personally approve every shipment, I said we couldn't accept an order on that basis.   I explained that we had to have a mutually acceptable **objective** standard any reasonable third-party could measure. But he still insisted on his subjective approval.

VP: What could you have done to uncover this problem before you went to all that trouble?

Sal: I really don't know.

VP: Okay. Tell me what led you to believe you would get the order if you met his Conditions of Satisfaction.

Sal: I started by saying, "If I show you a package you can ship your product in, and which will display the product as well as advertise it, what will you do?"

      He said he would give me an order if our price came in at $6 or $7 per unit. Our price came in at $5.85. But then he raised this color matching thing.

VP: Let me ask you again. What could you have done while you were negotiating his Conditions of Satisfaction to have this issue surface?

Sal: I don't know.

VP: When he gave you the wallpaper swatch and the ad, did you ask whether the colors were exactly what he wanted?

Sal: No. I figured that since he gave them to me, they were what he wanted.

VP: But you know from your training you can't rely on "I figured." The only commitments you can depend on are those that are clearly discussed and agreed upon. That's why we're so thorough when we negotiate the Conditions of Satisfaction.

Sal: I know, but sometimes I'm hesitant because I'm afraid the prospect will come up with a condition we can't meet. In traditional selling that would be an "objection." I was taught to avoid objections and "handle" them only if the prospect persists. You're saying we should raise them even when the prospect doesn't?

VP: Absolutely. Look how much time you spent because you didn't "handle the objection" up front. What would have happened if you had exposed the color problem before you did all the work?

Sal: You're right. I did waste a lot of time.

VP: Time is too valuable to waste. For that reason, being **thorough and precise** when you establish the customer's Conditions of Satisfaction is extremely important.

       How did you handle Conditions of Satisfaction with Chuck Riley from Target Brands?

Sal: When I asked him about his Conditions of Satisfaction, he looked at me like I was talking Latin. So I explained I would ask him some questions to determine exactly what he wanted and when I was done he could ask me any questions he had.

       My first question was what he wanted to accomplish by using an exterior package that doubled as a free-standing aisle display. He said his company was going to offer their retailers a twenty percent discount for a limited time, if the retailer would use an aisle display that passed the twenty percent discount on to the consumer. He expected the promotion to increase his market share with his existing retailers and probably get him some new business from retailers who weren't carrying his line.

       So I asked how much more he was willing to spend for new packaging? He said he could afford an additional $2.50 per carton. That settled price.

       Next I asked what kind of graphics he expected to get

for that price. He said he wanted a sixteen by twenty four-color header, with two-color lettering on the sides. Then I said, "What if you can only get one color lettering on the sides for that price?" He said, "I can live with it." I said, "Are you sure?" He said, "Yes, what's important is the header. It has to be printed in four colors." That handled graphics.

I asked whether they had their art work prepared and he said the mock-ups were approved and their ad agency would have the art work completed by the end of next week. I was on a roll.

When I asked him what quantity he would order, he said two thousand. I asked when he needed delivery and he said in about ten weeks. That took care of the delivery issue.

Moving right along, I asked what color packaging material he wanted and he said white.

Then I asked, "Is there anything else that's important to you?" He said the package had to be easy to set up and protect the merchandise as well as his current packaging does. So I asked to see what he had been using. He showed me a sample and after looking at it, I knew our packaging would satisfy that condition.

I asked him, "What else?" He said the colors had to meet industry specifications.

I said, "What else?" He said the packaging had to be easy for his production people to assemble, fill and seal.

I asked, "Anything else?" and he said, "No, that's it."

While we spoke I wrote every word down. Then I read

his conditions back to him and asked if I had them right. He said I did. So I said, "Are you sure that's all?" He said, "That's what I need."

So I asked, "If I come back in two weeks and demonstrate that we can meet all your Conditions of Satisfaction, what will you do?"

He said, "I'll see to it that you walk out of here with the purchase order in your hand."

Yesterday I went back with a sample of our standard aisle display packages and a quote. The first thing I did was read him his Conditions of Satisfaction and ask whether anything had changed since we made the list. He said, "Nothing has changed."

So I said, "When we met two weeks ago you said if we could meet your Conditions of Satisfaction you would give me an order today. Has that changed?" He said he would keep his promise. Then I told him there was one condition I couldn't meet exactly and asked if he was willing to discuss it. He said, "Of course." I explained that in order to give him a package that would fit and protect his merchandise, the four-color printed header would have to be fifteen by nineteen inches instead of sixteen by twenty.

He asked, "Why?" so I showed him on a sample that the graphics on the header wouldn't fit if they were as wide as the exterior dimensions of the package.

He said he was disappointed, but that he would probably accept it if everything else was right. I said, "What do you mean by 'probably'?"

He said he wanted to see the quote and a few other

items first. I said, "There's no sense doing anything else until this is resolved." Finally he said, "If everything else is satisfactory I'll accept the smaller header size. I said, "Are you sure?" He said, "Yes."

Then we reviewed every point, one at a time. When we were done I walked out with the order.

VP: Not bad for a beginner!

Sal: He even thanked me.

VP: Not unusual for a High Probability Salesperson. What did you say when he thanked you?

Sal: I said, "Thank you for your business."

VP: Your only mistake. Better to say, "You're welcome."

Sal: Why?

VP: Think about it.

CHAPTER TWELVE

A Complete High Probability Sale

Sal is on the phone at his desk prospecting from a new list of manufacturers.

Sal: Hello, Environmental Garden Products (EGP), I'd like to talk to the person in charge of packaging.(pause) Would you please connect me? (pause) Thank you.

Tom: Hello, Tom Merchant speaking.

Sal: Hello, this is Sal Esman from WPC packaging. We manufacture self-contained, four-color display packaging which is shipped flat and is easy to assemble. Is that something you want for your product line?

Tom: Do you mean the kind of boxes that double as point of sale displays?

Sal: That's right. Is that something you want?

Tom: Sounds like something we could use. I'd like to hear about it. We have a new product ready for package design and I'd like to use display packaging if it's cost effective and meets our other requirements. Can you come in next Monday and show me what you've got?

Sal: I'll be out of town Monday and Tuesday. How about Wednesday?

Tom: Wednesday works for me. What time?

Sal: Is nine in the morning okay?

Tom: See you at nine next Wednesday.

Sal: Tom, when we meet, if our packaging meets your criteria, what will you do?

Tom: We'll do some business together.

Sal: Please write my phone number down in case an emergency comes up and you can't keep the appointment.

Tom: Okay. Let me have your number.

The following Wednesday, Sal was waiting in the lobby of EGP when Tom Merchant came out to greet him.

Tom: Hello, you must be Sal. I'm Tom Merchant. Let's go into the conference room and you can show me what you've got.

Sal: Okay. (Following him into the office) Your company must be very busy. I had a hard time finding a parking spot in your lot.

Tom: We're very busy. The company has almost tripled since I started here.

Sal: When was that?

Tom: About nine years ago.

Sal: How long have you been the merchandising manager?

Tom: Almost four years.

Sal: What did you do before that?

Tom: I was the product manager for our insecticides line.

Sal: Is that how you started out with EGP?

Tom: No. I started here as a sales rep.

Sal: What did you do before you joined EGP?

Tom: I sold wholesale hardware for about three years.

Sal: Was that your first job?

Tom: No. My first job was the one just before that. I was a layout artist for an advertising agency.

Sal: That usually takes specialized training, doesn't it?

Tom: Yes, it does. My college degree was in art.

Sal: Where did you go?

Tom: I went to PCA.

Sal: Were you in Fine Art or Commercial?

Tom: Actually, my major was in Fine Art, but I took a lot of commercial courses too.

Sal: How come?

Tom: Well, my parents always said it would be tough to make a living selling fine art. They turned out to be right.

Sal: What do you mean?

Tom: I tried making a living as an artist for a while but it was too tough. I still paint in my spare time, but more for love than money.

Sal: What was tough about being an artist?

Tom: I painted for about four years. I was single at the time and barely made a living. Then I got married and our first daughter was born within a year. I had a family to support so I started free-lancing in commercial art. Then the advertising agency I mentioned, offered me a full-time position and I took it.

Sal: Who first noticed you had artistic talent?

Tom: My mother. She was a commercial artist. In fact, she still works about ten hours a week for some of her old clients.

Sal: When did she first realize you had talent?

Tom: I was about four. We were visiting my aunt for Christmas. There were a bunch of cousins who were all about my age. My aunt wanted the kids out of the way so she sent us down the basement with crayons and paper. I decided to draw each of my cousins. My cousin Susan brought her drawing upstairs and showed her parents. Then all the adults came down to watch me work. I think that's the first time I had any idea I could draw.

Sal: How did your father react?

Tom: My dad never had any appreciation for art. To him talents only matter if they can generate money. He equates how much talent you have with how much you make.

Sal: It sounds like the relationship with him was a little strained.

Tom: Still is. He still only wants to know how much money I earn.

Sal: Was he successful?

Tom: He's done quite well, financially, at least.

Sal: What do you mean?

Tom: Well, he's not a very happy guy. He's really a tough person to get along with.

Sal: In what way?

Tom: He's very demanding and it's hard for him to show affection.

Sal: Was he at the Christmas party where you drew the pictures of your cousins?

Tom: He was there. His remark was something like how hard it was to make a fortune as an artist.

Sal: How has that affected you?

Tom: I've always felt that my father didn't appreciate who I am. He's never been satisfied with anything I've accomplished.

Sal: How have you handled that?

Tom: For a long time I tried to impress him by excelling in whatever I did. Finally I just gave up.

Sal: Why?

Tom: That's a good question. (reflecting for a moment) I realized that no matter what I did, it wasn't going to be good enough. Then when I got older I realized he loved me and it was just hard for him to show it.

Sal: What happened?

Tom: Do you really want to hear this?

Sal: Yes.

Tom: Well, the day I left for college I was standing outside our house waiting for my ride and my father came outside and started to wish me luck. He got all choked up and couldn't finish what he was saying. He actually had tears in his eyes. Then he hugged me and walked back into the house without saying anything.

Sal: What was that experience like for you?

Tom: It really meant a lot to me. For the first time I began to understand who he was. I was really touched.

Sal: How does he get along with your children?

Tom: Incredibly well. He loves being with them and they're crazy about him.

Sal: What kind of relationship do you have with your kids?

Tom: I remember what went on for me, so I always try to show them I appreciate whatever they do. In fact, my wife and I make it a point not to show more enthusiasm for my younger daughter's artistic talents than we show the other kids. That's not easy for me, since I relate to her best.

Sal: How many children do you have?

Tom: I have three, two girls and a boy. The baby, Jeannie, is eighteen now. She's the artist. She could draw before she could write. Now she's winning prizes for her art at Bard College.

Sal: What talents do the other two have?

Tom: My older daughter, Nancy, was always a math student. She's a systems analyst for G.E. My son, Mike, is a carpenter.

Sal: How about your wife?

Tom: She's been a paralegal for years.

Sal: How does she feel about your art?

Tom: She's my biggest fan. She writes publicity releases about my work and gets them into the local newspaper. Most of the work I sell comes from that.

Sal: Sounds like you really appreciate her support.

Tom: I do. I appreciate it a lot. She's really a very special person.

Sal: Why do you say that?

Tom: She's a terrific wife, a good homemaker and a great mom. Just about everyone says they feel better when they're around her. Of course, on top of that, she earns a living and still has time to promote my paintings.

Sal: What would you do if you could make a living painting?

Tom: I'd probably quit my job and paint full-time.

Sal: (smiling) Then we'd better talk business now. When I
        called last week you said you had a new product that
        was ready for package-design and you wanted to
        combine packaging with point-of-sale advertising. Is that
        still what you want?

Tom: What you described on the phone sounded right for one
        of my new lines. I've seen that kind of exterior
        packaging before. It's obviously more expensive than
        what we use now. We're using plain corrugated
        packaging with stenciled lettering on the sides.

Sal: You're right. WPC packaging is more expensive. Why
        do you need four-color display packaging?

Tom: It's not like I need it. But we would like to upgrade our
        profile somewhat and increase our name recognition.

Sal: Do you want four-color display packaging?

Tom: Yes, if it increases sales.

Sal: Our packaging costs about two dollars more per package
        than what you're using now. Are you prepared to spend
        that?

Tom: If the new packaging improves sales by more than two
        percent, we would cover our costs and get the
        advertising we want virtually free.

Sal: Does that mean you're prepared to spend an additional
        two dollars a package, or not?

Tom: Yes, I am.

Sal: If you decided to go forward, when would you want the new packaging?

Tom: I'd need to have it on hand in about three months. That would give us about two weeks to work on assembly, packing and sealing. That way we could ship by the beginning of our next busy season.

Sal: What would happen if you didn't have the new packaging in three months?

Tom: Then we couldn't target a trial run for about another nine months. That's when our business peaks again.

Sal: When you're making a major decision like this, who else do you like to talk it over with?

Tom: Our sales manager is the person I talk to about things like this.

Sal: Then it's important I meet with him for about fifteen minutes to show him some samples, answer his questions and find out what his objectives are. That way I'll know I'm meeting everyone's criteria. Can you arrange that?

Tom: No problem. He approves major packaging changes, anyway.

Sal: If you decided to go forward, who else would have to agree?

Tom: The product manager and our advertising manager.

Sal: Okay, I'll need to talk to them too, to be sure that what we're doing meets with their approval. Are you willing to arrange that?

Tom: Sure. How's Friday morning?

Sal: Friday morning's not good for me. How about this Thursday or any day next week from Wednesday on?

Tom: How about a week from this Friday at 10 A.M.?

Sal: That's good. Now, suppose we meet and agree to go ahead, who would have to approve that decision?

Tom: The chief financial officer. He has to approve projects that don't have a proven financial track record.

Sal: Okay. We need to talk to your financial officer before we go any further. If he disapproves, we won't waste everyone's time. Can you find out if he'll see us now?

Tom: (picking up the phone) Hello, Bob, it's Tom. I have Sal Esman of WPC Packaging in my office. I'm considering a new exterior packaging that's designed and decorated to be converted into an aisle display by the retailer. Can we meet with you now for about ten minutes to get your approval for a test run? (pause) To see whether the concept makes economic sense. (pause) I think so. But I won't know for sure without putting some out there for a little while. That takes money, and your approval for a trial run. (pause) (to Sal) He wants to know how much a trial run will cost?

Sal: Tell him between $9,000 and $12,000.

Tom: (into the phone) Between $9,000 and $12,000. (pause) Okay, Bob. Thanks. Bye. (to Sal) He said he'll approve a maximum of $10,000. Can you do a test run for

$10,000?

Sal: I think we can. What would happen if you don't go ahead with this test?

Tom: I'm on the line to improve our market penetration. Right now your packaging looks promising. If I don't test yours I'll probably look to someone else's. I'd really like to know whether display packaging like yours can improve sales, so I'm anxious to see a pilot project in action.

Sal: If you had to decide right now, without talking to me or anyone else, whose packaging would you choose?

Tom: I really don't have a preference.

Sal: Is there someone you would rather do business with?

Tom: No. Obviously, our present suppliers don't offer your kind of product. If they did, we would've already tried it. I have spoken with a couple of other suppliers who do sell your kind of packaging.

Sal: Is there another supplier you prefer to do business with, or not?

Tom: No. If I preferred someone else I would've already given them the account.

Sal: What's your procedure for issuing a purchase order?

Tom: I write up a purchase requisition spelling out all the terms and conditions. Then the product manager and the CFO have to sign off on it. When they do, it goes to purchasing. If purchasing approves the terms and conditions, they formalize it. If they don't approve, the order comes back to me, and you and I have to meet with the purchasing manager to work out the problems.

Sal: Does that mean after we've done all the work the purchasing department can bring in another supplier?

Tom: No. If your company's reputation checks out, as long as your firm is technically and financially capable of handling the order, you'll get the order.

Sal: What would it mean to you if this didn't happen?

Tom: I have to justify my salary, like everyone else. If I'm not producing, I'm out of here; and like I said, I can't support my family on my art work.

Sal: Is there any reason you wouldn't want to do business with me? (pause) Something we haven't covered yet? (pause) An emotional reason? (pause) Anything?

Tom: No. In fact, you've really been a pleasure to deal with. If next Friday's meeting with my people goes just as well, I'm sure you'll get this order. I suggest, though, that you prepare a mockup of the design for the meeting; one that shows our product line.

Sal: I'll bring some sample displays we've made for other customers. They'll be the approximate size and design we discussed. If we glue some of your existing art work to the headers it'll make a serviceable presentation. But I'll need to see whether all your managers agree with the concept before I start making original mockups.

Tom: I really think you should have a finished mockup for the meeting.

Sal: I'm not willing to do all that work until I'm sure the project will go forward. Once I'm sure of that, I'll be happy to produce the mockup and a quotation.

Tom: Okay, I understand your position. You sure take a strong stand.

Sal: What could be lurking in the background that would prevent this from happening?

Tom: Nothing I know of. I think you've really covered all the bases.

Sal: If I can meet all your criteria for a new type of packaging, what will you do?

Tom: You've got a sale.

Sal: Okay, I'll see you on Friday morning.

FRIDAY:

During Friday's meeting, Tom Merchant confidently showed every key manager the stock packaging sample Sal made using a photocopy of EGP's proposed art work glued to the header. Everyone agreed that the aisle displays were worth testing. After the meeting, Sal and Tom went back to Tom's office.

Tom: Take a photocopy of the art work back to your people for the quotation. You can use it for the mockup too. How soon can you get me a quote?

Sal: I'll have it to you by Wednesday afternoon. But I have to establish your Conditions of Satisfaction before you and I go any further...

Tom: What do you mean by my "Conditions of Satisfaction"?

Sal: We need to discuss all the conditions that have to be met in order for us to do business.

Tom: Fire away.

Sal: First, assuming that WPC can meet your Conditions of Satisfaction, what will you do?

Tom: By Conditions of Satisfaction do you mean like price and delivery?

Sal: Not just price and delivery, but everything that's important to you about the packaging.

Tom: If you can satisfy all of my requirements, I'll give you the order.

Sal: Okay (taking out his notebook). Price first. You said you'll spend up to two dollars more than you're paying for your current packaging.

Tom: How do you know that?

Sal: I'm reading from the notes I took at our first meeting.

Tom: I wondered why you took all those notes. Looks like it pays to be thorough.

Sal: It's important to know what we can expect from each other. That way we both win - I get what I want and you get what you want. The best way I know to do that is to discuss in advance everything that's important.

Tom: Sounds good to me. Let's go.

Sal: When we first met you said you needed the packaging in three months. It's been two weeks since we had that conversation so I assume you need the packaging in eleven weeks. Is that right?

Tom: I'd really prefer delivery in ten weeks. That way we'll have some extra time to set up the production line.

Sal: Okay, we'll change that to ten weeks. But that's about the best we can do. I'll give you the actual dimensions of the assembled packages when I bring you the quote. The dimensions will be different from your current packaging. But the packages will hold the same amount of merchandise, thirty units per package. Is that okay?

Tom: It's okay if twenty of them fit on a standard pallet.

Sal: That'll work. The printing on the header will match your color specifications and deviations will be within industry standards. Is that okay?

Tom: I want the tolerances forty percent better than industry standards.

Sal: I can do that but that adds about fifty percent to the printing costs. Are you willing to pay more for the tolerances you want?

Tom: No. I can't pay extra for that. But if WPC does quality work, you should have no problem giving me the closer tolerances.

Sal: Our internal standards are actually tighter than what you're asking for. We always meet industry standards but we don't always meet our internal standards. We won't guarantee better than industry standards unless we charge for the extra quality controls and inspections we would need. What do you want to do?

Tom: Other salesmen have said their printing always beats industry standards by at least sixty percent.

Sal: If they can guarantee that quality at no additional cost, perhaps you should give them your business.

Tom: If I believed them, I would consider it. But they weren't willing to guarantee it, even with an additional charge. You're being straight with me and I like that. I get tired of hearing people promise the finest possible quality and the lowest possible price.

Sal: So what do you want to do?

Tom: I'll have to accept your standard quality.

Sal: Tom, you don't have to do anything you don't want to do.

Tom: Well, that's what I want to do.

Sal: Are you sure?

Tom: I'm sure.

Sal: What colors do you want for the exterior?

Tom: Can you print a deep purple and black on standard buff stock?

Sal: No problem.

Tom: The header, of course, has to be on white glossy stock.

Sal: Right.

Tom: What about material thickness?

Sal: Our packaging will be thicker than what you're using now, and that'll make each package a little heavier. I'll give you the exact thickness in the quotation. Is that acceptable?

Tom: That's fine.

Sal: I'll need a case of merchandise to work with. I'll bring it back with the quote. Can you do that?

Tom: No problem.

Sal: Now let's handle payment terms. The quote will call for one-third, thirty days after the order is accepted and the balance, net thirty from day of delivery. Is there any problem with that?

Tom: As long as your first bill is identified as "set-up charges," it's okay.

Sal: I'll see to it. What else?

Tom: We only handle packaging materials that are palletized to standard pallets, covered with clear plastic and strapped in place. Overall height can't be more than forty-eight inches. We keep the pallets.

Sal: Agreed. What else?

Tom: We won't accept deliveries more then two days ahead of schedule. If you're going to be late you have to notify us at least one week in advance. But I don't have to tell you, you'll probably kill the whole thing if you're late on this first run.

Sal: Understood.

Tom: Also, I think I'll need a WPC representative on site when we first set up the new production line.

Sal: My best guess is it'll only take about half an hour to show your people how to assemble the packages.

Tom: You don't know our people, but I don't think a half hour will do it on my end. Figure on half a day.

Sal: Okay. I'll try to be available myself for a half-day, at most, and I think I can do it in less.

Tom: Another thing, Sal. It's important that we not spend any more time on assembly than we do now.

Sal: I'll demonstrate that our packages can be assembled at least as fast as your current packaging, but that's as far as I can take it.

Tom: Understood.

Sal: Fine. So if I show you and your assembly people that the new packages can be assembled at least as fast as your current packaging, will that be acceptable?

Tom: Yes.

Sal: What else?

Tom: I can't think of anything else.

Sal: I'm trying to anticipate every problem now so we can handle them before they happen.

Tom: That's been obvious from the start. But I think I'm finally fresh out of what you call "Conditions of Satisfaction."

Sal: If you think of any others, call me before Wednesday.

Tom: Okay. I'll see you then.

THE FOLLOWING WEDNESDAY:

Sal came to Wednesday's meeting with a large square package, wrapped in brown paper.

Tom: Is that the mockup?

Sal: Yes. And I have the quotation too. But before...

Tom: (interrupting) Let me see the mockup first.

Sal: Before we look at the mockup, we need to review your Conditions of Satisfaction to be sure that the quote and the mock-up conform. (taking out his notebook) First, the total price for the initial order cannot exceed $10,000. Correct?

Tom: Correct.

Sal: And the price per piece can't be more than two dollars higher than your current packaging.

Tom: Right.

Sal: Delivery has to be completed within ten weeks.

Tom: Right, and delivery has to be on time or no more than two days early.

Sal: Right. Next, the packages must hold thirty units of product and fit twenty packages to a pallet.

Tom: Okay, so far.

Sal: You want the packages shipped flat, on standard-sized wood pallets, covered with clear plastic and strapped to the pallets. The loaded pallets can't be more than forty-eight inches high.

Tom: Right.

Sal: The printing must meet industry standards for color fidelity.

Tom: That's okay for the specified colors. But we didn't discuss the fidelity for the four-color graphics on the header.

Sal: I'll make a note. We can discuss that after we confirm the rest of the points. Next you said you wanted standard buff stock with black and deep purple printing for the exterior of the box.

Tom: Correct.

Sal: We agreed that the surface of the header will be white glossy.

Tom: Right.

Sal: I told you the weight will be heavier than your current stock.

Tom: Why does it have to be heavier if it holds the same thirty units our current packages hold?

Sal: Because these packages don't just get emptied and trashed. These are aisle displays that have to stand upright on the floor. The header is elevated to eye level.

Most importantly, they have to withstand shopping carts, feet and kids.

Tom: Say no more.

Sal: You agreed to pay for the set up charges, one-third within thirty days after acceptance, and the balance net thirty days.

Tom: Right.

Sal: You also need me, or another WPC representative, to show your production line people how to assemble and load the packages.

Tom: For at least half a day.

Sal: Tom, I believe that was, "at most" half a day.

Tom: Well, what if we have problems?

Sal: Let's stick with what we agreed to until I finish the list. Then we can discuss any changes, okay?

Tom: Fair enough.

Sal: Along those same lines, we agreed if I can demonstrate that the assembly can be done as fast as the old packages, that would meet your assembly line time requirement.

Tom: Right.

Sal: Okay, that's the entire list of your Conditions of Satisfaction. Has anything changed since we agreed on that list, or is there anything you've thought of since then you want to add?

Tom: Only that the price per piece for future orders of the same quantity stays the same.

Sal: For now the answer is yes. But future orders have to be subject to inflation.

Tom: I'm concerned about the price going up more than the rate of inflation.

Sal: Why are you concerned about that?

Tom: Because of the ten thousand dollar limit my CFO put on this order. Your strategy could be to increase the price on the next order.

Sal: Do you think I would do that without discussing it with you?

Tom: No, I don't think you would. But I don't know WPC's management. They might.

Sal: Even if they would, and I can tell you they don't do business that way, I would come to you first.

Tom: So you're telling me not to worry about that, right?

Sal: Right. Is the list I just read exactly what we agreed to?

Tom: Yes. But we still have a couple of questions.

Sal: Assuming we get those questions settled so that we're both satisfied, what will you do?

Tom: I'll fill out the requisition today and you'll get the purchase order by Friday.

Sal: Okay. Now let's deal with your questions. About color

fidelity, I thought when we said "colors" we meant all colors, including the colors on the four-color picture. What did you mean?

Tom: I don't think industry standards are clear on "brightness."

Sal: Suppose you give me two samples printed on standard photographic paper, one that's the dullest acceptable and one that's the brightest. I'm sure we can produce within that range and they'll be our standards.

Tom: That's easy. I can have our photo people do that right now. Can you meet a five percent brightness deviation?

Sal: No, but I can guarantee seven percent.

Tom: Okay, I can live with seven percent.

Sal: The other open point from your original list of Conditions of Satisfaction is how long you'll need a WPC representative to train your production line people.

Tom: Understand, I'm just concerned that something might go wrong.

Sal: If something goes wrong and it's our fault, someone will stay until the problem's corrected. But getting your line up and running with the new package shouldn't take more than an hour, if you have all the materials in place and the line cleared before we start.

Tom: I understand. But just in case something does go wrong, will you or someone else stay until we're running?

Sal: As long as you start on time.

Tom: Good. I appreciate that.

Sal: Have I covered your Conditions of Satisfaction completely?

Tom: You have. Now let me see the mockup.

Sal removed the wrapping and assembled the package. The box was square and open at the top. The EGP logo and the product name were lettered on all four sides in black and purple on a white background. A white cardboard header extended about sixteen inches above the top. The header had a laminated four-color process poster on its front.

Tom: It looks terrific. But the dimensions are not what I expected. It's almost square. Even with the header raised it'll be too low to catch the customer's eye when it's placed in a store aisle.

Sal: The display box has to be set up on top of an unopened box. That's how you get the height.

Tom: Okay, I see. But what happens when the retailer only has one box left.

Sal: The retailer has to save an empty box and put the display on top of it.

Tom: That's easy enough. I see you used white stock for the mock-up, but I thought we would use a buff stock for production to keep the cost down.

Sal: You're right to an extent. In standard weights, buff costs a lot less because it's manufactured in huge quantities. But in the heavier weights we use for these display packages, there's not much difference in cost. White adds only about two percent to the total cost.

Tom: Did you quote it in white?

Sal: I actually quoted it both ways. Let's look at the quote. The price for setting up the job (handing Tom a copy of the quote) is $2,400. The price per package for the initial lot of 2,000 pieces on white stock is $3.72.

Tom: That totals $9,840. You just made it under $10,000. Does that include shipping?

Sal: Yes. The quote is a delivered price. If we use buff-colored stock, the price per package is about two percent less.

Tom: I'm surprised. The price per-piece is only $1.78 more than the corrugated boxes we're using now. Are future orders at the same price per-piece, without set-up charges of course?

Sal: Yes, subject to inflation, provided you don't change the dimensions or the art work. You can count on delivery ten weeks from receipt of the executed order.

Tom: Then I'd better get my order out by Friday. It looks like everything meets my Conditions of Satisfaction.

I'll get you the four color art work samples so we can both sign them. I'll get two sets completed while we go to lunch so you can take them with you today.

I'll put a four hour time requirement on the purchase order for training our production line people. Can we have a private understanding that you'll do everything within reason to see to it that everything goes well?

Sal: Yes.

Tom: Good. Let me order the prints and dictate the requisition. Then we can go to lunch. You have a new customer. Thanks.

Sal: You're welcome.

AFTERWORD

This is not intended to be a how-to book or an all inclusive text. It is not likely you will become proficient in High Probability Selling merely by reading about it. Learning High Probability Selling generally requires about thirty-six hours of rigorous interactive classroom time and a desire to be better than pretty good at what you do.

High Probability, Inc., conducts sales training for individuals in Philadelphia, Pennsylvania. Corporate training is usually conducted on-site.

High Probability, Inc., is located in Langhorne, Pennsylvania and can be reached at 215-968-8827 in Pennsylvania and at 800-394-7762 outside of Pennsylvania. The fax number is 215-968-2983. The e-mail address is *HiProbSell@aol.com.* Our World Wide Web site is *http://www.HighProbSell.com.*

I want information about:

[ ] HIGH PROBABILITY SALES TRAINING
     FOR INDIVIDUALS

[ ] HIGH PROBABILITY SALES TRAINING
     FOR CORPORATIONS

[ ] BOOK ON TAPE

Name _____

Company_____

Street_____

Town _____ State _____ Zip _____

Phone (_____)_____

Fax   (_____)_____

You can write us at:

       High Probability, Inc.
       206 South Chancellor Street
       Newtown, PA   18940

Or call (215) 968-8827 in PA. and
800-394-7762 outside of PA.

Our e-mail address is *HiProbSell@aol.com.*

ORDER FORM

HIGH PROBABILITY SELLING $19.95

Telephone orders: 1-800-394-7762
    Have your VISA or MasterCard ready when you call.

FAX orders: (215) 968-2983 Credit Card orders only.

Postal orders: High Probability, Inc.
                      206 S. Chancellor Street
                      Newtown, PA   18940

Sales tax: In Pennsylvania please include 6% sales tax.

Shipping: Priority Mail: $4.00 per book.

Payment: [ ]   Check
        Credit card: [ ] MasterCard   [ ] VISA

    Card Number: _____

    Name on Card: _____

    Exp. date: _____

Name: _____

Address: _____

            _____

Phone #   _____

Price subject to change without notice.